EVERYBODY WINS!

To my father,
who worked for a dream and gave me a cause;
and to my family, and to all of our children
who will have a future in America
bright with opportunities.

EVERYBODY WINS!

Stephen J. Cabot

HIPPOCRENE BOOKS
New York

Acknowledgments

I would like to express my appreciation to all my colleagues at Pechner, Dorfman, Wolffe, Rounick & Cabot who helped me make this possible. I have gained valuable insights from all of them and profited from their deep knowledge of labor relations. This book could not have been written without their encouragement and support.

I am particularly indebted to Rusch O. Dees, Esquire, and David M. Schloss, Esquire, for their invaluable contributions, and to Herbert Abramson for editorial assistance.

Finally, I wish to thank the secretarial staff of Pechner, Dorfman, Wolffe, Rounick & Cabot who labored over the manuscript from rough draft to final edition.

Stephen J. Cabot

Philadelphia, Pennsylvania
January, 1986

For information, address: Hippocrene Books,
171 Madison Avenue, New York, NY 10016.

Printed in the United States of America.

Contents

Introduction   vii

Part One: The Evolution and the Challenge

I.	The Widening Breach	3
II.	Do Concessions Work?	17
III.	Brawlers with Blinders	35
IV.	Government and Labor: An International Scorecard	47
V.	How to Ignore the Lessons of History	63
VI.	The Nonunion World	79
VII.	The New Face of the Labor Force — Opportunities and Dangers	91

Part Two: The Vital New Direction

VIII.	Needed: A Continuity for Courage	109
IX.	For Business: New Criteria and New Judgments	129
X.	For Labor: A Partnership Rather Than an Adversarial Relationship	143
XI.	Productivity, Robotics, Or —?	161
XII.	Clearing the Air with New Semantics	175
XIII.	A How-to-Do-It for the Nonunion Company	183
XIV.	Collective Leadership vs. Collective Bargaining	201

Index   213

INTRODUCTION

"We must all hang together, or assuredly we shall all hang separately."
— *Benjamin Franklin*

Why bother?
With today's frostily congealed attitudes between American management and American labor, it seems reasonable to wonder why anyone would try to melt those attitudes and remove the frost. One would need to pry away many decades of prejudice, protective layers, and political veneers to be able to get at the human beings underneath. Is it worth it and is it possible?

This book, two years in the writing and reflective of twenty years experience in management-labor turmoil, is dedicated to that effort. The needs are urgent; the time is fleeting and the challenges facing our country hardly leave the opportunity to idle along in the same syndrome of management-labor strife and economic malaise which that creates. We just cannot muddle along anymore.

I am thoroughly convinced that management and labor must end their destructive, adversarial relationship. They must together attack our problems of frequent high unemployment, reduced productivity, technological decline, fading international presence, and class divisiveness. There is no time left for the autocratic, unilateral behavior of those who run business and those who run labor which has resulted in the rigid confrontation and bad blood that characterize today's relations.

Business and labor must join in collective leadership instead of their long, unproductive adversarial tradition.

Hang-tough policies on both sides, management and labor stubborness, union concessions under pressure, lack of communication within each side and between each other, scare tactics, hiring of unskilled industrial relations people who are only meant to go through the motions, and excessive union demands which are only designed to help the current union officials stay entrenched — none of these have worked. It's no longer a matter of anyone being pro-management or pro-labor but of everyone being pro-America. And if that sounds like super-nationalism, jingoism, or whatever, so be it.

A detailed and careful effort has been made throughout this book to describe, first, the evolution and challenge of our nation's management-labor relationship, and, second, the vital new direction so urgently needed. Many examples derived from my own experience as a management-labor relations attorney are presented to portray the good and bad effects which have been experienced in the field. And, most important, suggestions are offered for new ways in which business and labor can conduct themselves for the greater good, for their mutual benefit, and particularly for the reinvigoration and progress of our national economy.

Pains have been taken to analyze the trend of labor concessions; how our government's labor relations policies stack up with those of other nations; the world of non-union companies; the new face of the labor force; the challenge of robotics; and the need for management and labor to develop a new semantics.

All incidents which I describe are true. Fictional episodes in Chapters I and XIV are described as "fantasy" and are used only to dramatize the urgent need for a drastic change in our management-labor philosophies. One might call these fantasies, perhaps, polemical license.

Certainly, after many years in what may be one of the toughest roles in our society, I am well aware that much of what I say and advocate here will be attacked, scorned, and perhaps painted in suspicious terms. I am ready to accept that. I am convinced that out of sincerity, experience, and steadfastness, progress can be made. But the stakes are too high to be thin-skinned, or shy. One has to speak out in the interest of constructive harmony or accept the inevitable. We simply cannot allow our country to fall further into the morass of eroding productivity and fading international competitiveness. No one else can do it for us. It has to come from within to have any lasting meaning.

Why bother?

Why not, if we love our families, our children, our country? What some may not realize is that the needless strife and rancor of employers and employees can reach that deeply, that vitally into those most precious elements of our lives.

S.J.C.

PART ONE

THE EVOLUTION AND THE CHALLENGE

CHAPTER I

THE WIDENING BREACH

"Capitulate. There's nothing you can do. The union is too strong. Nobody — nobody — can fight it."

When you hear those words and see that the bitter eyes and anguished face of the person speaking them belong to your own father, you aren't likely to forget them. In fact, the words tend to burn into your memory and eventually push you into action.

That, simplistic as it may sound, is what happened to me. People see me now as a staid member of the conservative legal profession, but a fire is burning inside me and it has been burning for a long time.

For years my father successfully operated a diaper delivery service in our home city of Philadelphia. His trucks served families in the city, southern New Jersey, eastern Pennsylvania, and Wilmington, Delaware. His company was under contract to a union affiliated with the International Brotherhood of Teamsters, and he seemed to have labor problems continuously. He suffered through strikes, both actual and threatened, from the early 1950s through

1975. Generally, when he granted the wage increases that the union demanded, he passed on some of the higher costs to his customers. But the union squeeze play bothered him. "Some day," he warned the union's business agent, "you are going to price me out of the market and we'll both be sorry."

Eventually new technology in the form of paper diapers and the persistent militancy of the Teamsters' affiliate proved too much for him. He developed bleeding ulcers. As we sat at the dinner table, I remember him saying, "Well, there's no place for me to turn. My lawyer just sits there and doesn't do anything. One more increase like this last one and I'm finished." I also recall earlier times when he confided his troubles to his family, and I, still a child, imagined myself a knight on a white horse, a legal champion carrying the torch of troubled businessmen against big, bad unions. But his statement, "There's no place for me to turn," proved prophetic. Ultimately he had no recourse. Priced out of the market, he was forced to sell the business at a sizable loss.

My father's difficulties shaped my life. I knew from the time I was a teenager what I had to do. And at that I was lucky. I didn't suffer from the career confusion that many young people do. After Villanova University, I attended the University of Pennsylvania Law School. During the summer I clerked for a local law firm. My direction was set as though it were carved in stone. I would be the management-labor lawyer "with guts" whom my father so desperately needed.

In the nearly two decades since I hung out my "shingle," my objective hasn't changed one iota. This is true, despite hundreds of incidents in which I walked through angry pickets to help a harassed employer or sat across the table from red-faced, sputtering union officials. My objective hasn't changed although I was spat at, had my life threatened, found my car dented and its tires slashed. There have been times when I was called in to fight a union threat when it was almost too late to save the company. Union officials have used the media to heap such encomiums upon me as "the biggest, no-good union-busting SOB who ever lived." Through it all my goal has remained steadfast because I know that I am righting a wrong, balancing the scales. My goal is to provide management — even small employers with less than fifty workers — some measure of the clout which local affiliates of cash-rich national labor unions generate against them.

You might think that I should be staunchly antiunion. I may have started out that way, but I'm not any longer. I'm convinced that we must establish a balanced, productive relationship between American management and labor which allows both to live together and thrive. Intransigent, hang-tough policies of both business and labor hurt everyone — employers, workers, and the public at large. We are all affected.

First, let's take the employers.

In 1979, I helped a client who owns a General Motors dealership in Mount Holly, New Jersey, when his employees, members of a Teamsters Local, went on strike. I advised him on various options open to him. He chose to reject the union's demands for more money. After the strike had been under way for a while, he had to hire replacements for the twenty-four striking salesmen in order to survive. Without a sales staff, he would have been forced out of business. After some weeks the new workers petitioned the National Labor Relations Board to hold an election to oust the striking union. The Federal agency postponed releasing the results of the election, but eventually it became obvious that the union had lost. The strikers tendered their resignations and stopped picketing. It was all over.

"It was like David and Goliath," my client told a newspaper reporter afterward. "Unions literally hold an ax over business-men's heads. I needed somebody to help me."

Indeed, a great many employers can just about feel the union ax, the threat of a strike, coming down on them whenever it comes time to negotiate a labor contract. Employers want strikes as much as swimmers want to catch sight of sharks. But employers frequently cannot afford the demands unions make, which are rarely, if ever tied to increases in productivity. So employers are forced to choose between refusing demands they cannot afford and facing the hardships that strikes bring or yielding and operating at reduced profits or at a loss. Many times they buy labor peace at ridiculous prices, hoping that business will improve and absorb the added expense. But if profits do not increase, they are out of luck.

Fortunately, the Mt. Holly case worked out well for the employer. The *Wall Street Journal* of November 19, 1979, featured the story on page one under the headline "Labor Nemesis. When the Boss Calls in This Expert, the Union May Be in Real Trouble."

My father, needless to say, was very proud. I was happy, of course, because I did well for my client. Even more gratifying was the fact that the newspaper had recognized the value of a new type of management-labor lawyer so badly needed to curb the abuses of big labor. Later many other media and major television talkshows also covered my activities. The time for the management-labor advocate, it seems, had arrived.

Second, let's take a hard look at the unions themselves.

The plain fact is that unionism is very much on the decline. In the last three decades union membership has dropped from about 38 percent of the nation's work force to less than 19 percent, a decline of exactly one half. The reasons for the drop include the closing of many plants, the movement of factories to the South, where organizing has been notably unsuccessful, and the presence of younger, more independent workers whose ranks include minorities. In addition, internecine union turmoil has taken its toll. The aging union bosses made unrealistic demands on management to quell the rumblings of revolt from younger, more militant, more sophisticated members. In short, the unions just haven't gotten their act together in years. But unions were never more out of step with reality than in the period 1980–1982, years of deep economic recession when business most needed cooperation from labor.

I am not exaggerating when I report that many times union leaders have confided to me that they had "to go through the motions of hanging tough" just to satisfy their own members or superiors. But too often this rigid posture has led to strikes and to correspondingly inflexible reactions from management, with the result that union members and their families have been hurt.

While I certainly don't claim to be working for labor, I think unions have got to stop cultivating adversarial attitudes. Creating an "us against them" attitude harms both management and union members. Union leaders must give more realistic information to their members so that they can be in a position to judge the issues and not just accept politicized recommendations from the top. Younger members should be allowed more responsibility within locals and also within the larger scope of big unions.

It's my conviction that people like me, so-called "hardballers," provide an element of difference in the management-labor process which ultimately benefits the individual union member as much as management. We "hardballers" keep employers from yielding to impossible demands that drive up prices and render companies uncompetitive. While we may deny unions their latest round of demands we also keep businesses solvent. Solvent businesses mean employment for workers.

Put another way, unionism is fighting for its life if membership erosion persists. The cause of the erosion is neither management abuses nor the hard dealing of management-labor lawyers. Unions must look to their own policies before they can stop their losses.

Let's also look beyond business and labor, let's look at the nation. Why is my message so important to the public at large?

That's really the big question, the big issue. If I may be indulged, I would like to sketch this imaginary but not so unlikely scenario for the years ahead. . . .

Imagine a time when the smokestacks do not belch black, or even white smoke anymore, and the rivers and lakes are no longer yellow. Sophisticated pollution controls built into the manufacturing process have removed the chemical poisons before they even get to the environment. But in the plants another sort of poison brews. This poison consists of anger and dissatisfaction.

Initially there are a few slowdowns and lots of rank and file grousing. Absenteeism and petty sabotaging of equipment increase. Union givebacks of wages and benefits have left a sour taste in the mouths of the workers on the assembly line. Their faces are hardened and angry. Production stutters along, interrupting some months of hopeful improvement.

Then, in Gary and Pittsburgh, historically the focal points of strife, incidents erupt. A plant manager loses his self-control with a pair of slow-moving workers and a brief but bloody fight follows. In another plant a worker is slightly hurt. The foreman reacts by reproving the worker. There is a butting of heads and shoulders; two men are knocked down in the confrontation — and the plant lurches to a halt. The industrial relations manager calls a meeting with the union local's general executives. The heat of the fight sweeps them all into a nasty shouting match. The NLRB, shorn of its locks years ago, orders a hearing. Management appears. But the union, having lost many times in recent Board hearings, boycotts this one.

The NLRB cites the union and orders its regional leader to appear in a test case. Sensing more than a minor controversy, the media play up the incident and the matter gets national exposure. The union's national chiefs want to fight the case all the way. But the union's chief lobbyist in Washington warns flatly: "Be careful. There's a helluva lot more here than meets the eye. My spies tell me that the President this morning ordered the Labor Board chairman to use this incident to slap the whole labor movement. The idea is to demonstrate that national productivity is the highest priority and no union shenanigans will be condoned. Who knows, it could be that labor's rights are on the brink of destruction."

At the requested Board hearing the union bigwigs appear in force. The Board's examiner finds the local union guilty of a number of violations of the Federal Labor Act, as the union had expected. But instead of a hand slap or token fine, the examiner levies an unprecedented fine of $1 million on the union local. Condemning the fine as "a clear provocation," the union contingent storms out.

In Washington the next day the officials meet with the executive board of the AFL-CIO. Although the meeting is chaotic, there is general agreement that the provocation must be met in kind. The union chiefs order a three-day walkout for all unionized workers across the country.

Everywhere union members debate the issue. What is behind it all? Is it a manipulated conspiracy to turn American against American, workers against employer, neighbor against neighbor? In union families there are bitter disputes. In plants, arguments flare up among union members and even among nonunion people. Why was a union local punished so harshly? Did the White House order the judgment? Among management the questioning and the concern are no less intense. But as the day nears, a preliminary count indicates that at least 3.5 million union members will go out, in effect paralyzing the country.

In the White House the President huddles with his cabinet. It is a unique national emergency, the first time that the United States has faced a general strike. All agree that the timing couldn't be worse. Industrial productivity had raised hopes by showing some gain after years of decline. With a businessman at its head, the

Administration had pressed for an improvement in productivity as a means of shoring up the national defense and the economy.

"What worries the hell out of me," says the President, "is that with the country about to go on its knees for three days, there is a unique opportunity for a terrorist attack or a military strike against us. Who knows what some hothead group will do? What started all this, anyway?"

The Labor Secretary shrugs, but the Commerce Secretary speaks up. "The labor movement is shaken up, Mr. President," he says. "They have lost membership and they feel put upon by the tough stance of business. Since the early eighties the union members haven't gotten back what they gave up in concessions. I think, too, that they are tired of being blamed for the productivity lag. There's a hell of a lot of bitterness out there."

"You should know," the Labor Secretary says bitterly to the Commerce Secretary. "You were the one who convinced the President to pull the teeth of the NLRB."

"All right, that's enough!" snaps the President. "Mr. Labor Secretary, I want you to phone the president of the AFL-CIO and tell him I want him in my office at nine in the morning!"

When they meet, the President explains the situation and bluntly announces, "There are about twenty-one hours left before this walkout of yours starts. I want you to go on national television in the next few hours and call off the strike in the interest of national security. And then I want a thirty-day moratorium on any slowdown or stoppage while we talk it out."

The union veteran stares beyond the President and says, "I still like to think that this is a democracy. We will not surrender the only real weapon we have."

As he leaves the White House, a battery of cameras focuses on him. The union man's upheld right arm with clenched fist flashes across millions of television screens.

Starting on schedule, the walkout spreads quickly across the country. Major industries grind to a halt. Under White House orders, units of the U.S. Army descend upon plants, union offices, and the homes of the union officials. The confrontation has gone wildly out of control.

It is the nation's second Civil War.

Fantasy, you say? Perhaps. But how great is the distance from fantasy to reality? A blink of the eye, a heartbeat, a twist of fate, or the stubborn unwillingness to accept the obvious. Even an honest intention to pierce the veil between fancy and fact can be halfhearted. As Samuel Hoffenstein, the American humorist and poet, put it, "Little by little we subtract faith and fallacy from fact, the illusory from the true, and starve upon the residue." In other words, stripping the facts to the bone to get rid of the fantasy won't necessarily provide understanding.

What is missing from the process, perhaps, is to look squarely at some facts, set them against a basic misconception, and then draw a conclusion and a new direction from them both.

Facts: Since the late 1950s, the American economy has teetered on a precipice. Productivity, technological lead, research and development outlays, management skills, and multinational achievements all have woefully tumbled from previous heights. If all of those trends are left unchecked, the country's decline among the major developed nations can be disastrous, despite the importance of a strong dollar and low inflation. From the standpoint of international competition, our industrial problems are already well advanced.

Misconception: One could say that here is a real fantasy. As in the astrospace shoot-outs of recent movies, the hero — Mr. America — will inevitably surmount all obstacles and emerge triumphant. Otherwise put, the corporate chief executive in his chauffeured limo, his company's banner unfurled, will come hurtling into the fray. He will elbow aside foreign competitors, help to balance the Federal budget, apply his great skills and rugged mentality to revive industrial output, aid the government's struggle with social problems, and, almost as a by-product, propel his company to its previous heights. And unionized labor will overlook its increasing frustration and anger to join with management in all these tasks, hoping against hope that its millions of members will benefit from it all.

Conclusion: It will never happen. Astonishingly, at a time when other major countries which compete with the U.S. are benefiting either from a close, working harmony among government, business, and labor or from enlightened labor involvement in business policy, the management-labor schism in the U.S. has never been greater. Here business blames unions for lower productivity and years of inflation. Unions blame the declines in productivity, international competitiveness, innovation, and economic growth on cautious, greedy, crony-ridden management policies.

Direction: Obviously, as even the worst diehards must concede, a new, working harmony is vital. A cohesive rapport between the two opposing sides is absolutely necessary to carry forward a mutual objective of reversing the American economic decline. The challenge is a complex one, requiring new thinking and a new judgment process on the part of both American management and labor.

The crisis is here and the time is now.

Currently management and labor are like two dogs viciously snapping at each other. Moments after President Ronald Reagan's State-of-the-Union address in January 1983, two aging men on opposite sides of the industrial bargaining table demonstrated just how far apart labor and management were.

It was a moment when they should have responded to the troubled President's call for new efforts to turn around the still lagging economy. "Tell your workers not to seek wage increases higher than the rate of productivity!" snapped John Swearingen, chairman of the board of Standard Oil of Indiana, as he appeared on a nationally televised midnight talk and call-in show. "Tell your people not to take advantage of my people!" retorted William W. Winpisinger, president of the International Machinists' Union. The ensuing exchange was a flurry of charges and countercharges. The host, Phil Donahue, could only look on helplessly as his guests generated heat rather than shed light.

That incident was just another example of the adversarial nature of American management-labor relations. In the last decade and a half the American economy has gone on a roller coaster ride, largely due to the bad judgment of both management and labor. Much of that bad judgment can be attributed to the lack of understanding each side showed to the other. When labor was strong, it sought wages and benefits far greater than lagging productivity warranted. Management miscalculated and assumed that it wouldn't have to face up to the excessive demands of labor because it could pass on those costs to the public in the form of higher prices, as it did from the 1950s through the early 1970s. But both camps were not seeing clearly or reading one another correctly. High inflation, deepening recession, and an unfavorable trade balance hurt basic industries. These conditions, combined with double-digit interest rates, stunted the growth of the automotive, steel, housing, and household-durables industries, forcing a severe profit squeeze, production cuts, and the highest unemployment in decades.

The antagonism between management and labor didn't change much by 1985 when the country seemed to have revived economically and people were wondering whether the combination of low inflation, low interest rates, and low unemployment didn't augur for a continuation of better times.

So what happened? — a spate of strikes and near strikes. There were stoppages at both TWA and United Airlines, a New York hospital strike and a New York hotel strike. At the New York Stock Exchange, a strike threat went down to the wire before there was agreement between management and labor. Nor was there any lack of teachers' strikes. The school children of Chicago faced picketing teachers for the third time in three years. Across the country school boards and teachers' unions self-rightously blamed each other for empty classrooms. Perhaps one could only conclude that, good times or bad, the implacable adversary relationship just won't change.

Isn't it therefore vital to have a management-labor detente?

I have seen the need for detente growing over the twenty years that I have watched business giving away more than it could afford and mortgaging its future in order to keep labor happy in the present. I have seen labor giving in too many times in order to maintain harmony with businessmen who had no intention of returning the concessions. And I have seen too many businesses going down the drain because of intransigence on one side, the other side, or both sides. Having sympathy or understanding for the other side was considered softheaded. And I have seen men, women, and their families financially strapped, their life savings slipping away because those who run businesses and those who work for them were just too stubborn to show some plain common sense.

For years I felt as though I were a remote island in a sea, alone in the management-labor field. My approach was to play hardball. Lawyers on both sides were reluctant to fight, leaving the rhetoric and blows to the businessman and his lieutenants on the one side and to the union business agents and the workers on the other. For years a part of the legal community behaved as "a community of brothers," making deals for their clients which really helped no one. I am not opposed to deals, but when they are made at any cost, they simply don't work.

It hasn't been easy for me as a pro-employer labor attorney to realize that detente between both sides is absolutely necessary. Unions, understandably, haven't demonstrated much affection for me. I have been threatened many times, even warned that my house would be bombed. Pickets have followed me. But I have persisted — yes, hardballing — in serving a summons to a union leader on a picket line for contempt or arrest or handing him an injunction paper. I have also been told by other management-labor lawyers that my methods were too drastic. Some would warn businessmen not to hire me. A union business agent informed me that "if you don't back off and get the company to back off, you're gonna have trouble walking again." I told him, "Well, you'll have to do what you have to do and I'll do what I have to do." This exchange occurred during a brutal trucking strike in which there were shootings, bombings, and picket line violence. But when it was over, the same union official came to me and offered me a job representing his and other union locals. It was hardly an extensive conversation, but it ended with this comment: "Anyone as tough as you should be on the union's side, not management's."

I may have provoked some of the bitterness and harsh reaction. More than once I have deliberately driven past a group of pickets and parked at the boss's door. I was not shy about it. I represented the employer and did not see why I should conceal that fact just to curry the union's favor. I suppose it was also my way of registering my independence. At least everyone knew where I stood.

What I really believe, however, might have surprised many of those sullen pickets and their union leaders. I think we *can* get together, business and labor, and the lawyers on both sides, for the common good. In fact, not only can we, but we must.

Over the years in which I have represented management, regardless of whether or not a union was involved, I have been erroneously called a "union buster" simply because I represent management. But I am no more a union buster than Lane Kirkland, the head of the AFL-CIO, is a company buster. Just as Kirkland would not want to see the demise of the Chrysler Corporation, so have I no desire to see the United Auto Workers Union become extinct.

I did not come quickly to the realization that a new climate of management-labor rapport was vital. My thoughts evolved over the years until one day I saw the light. Sometimes, when one is embroiled in the heat of confrontation and dispute, the truth isn't as apparent as it should be. You could be too close to the battle to perceive why you are at war. In my case, it began to dawn on me that when there is one strike after another and litigation drags on, management and labor are unproductively flailing away at each other and really getting nowhere. No one is winning. Perhaps it's just the lawyers who are the winners. But the problem with any lingering labor dispute is that there remains bitterness which merely sets the stage for the next confrontation.

So can a management-labor attorney like me undergo enough of a change of heart to urge that the only way to win is through a combined management-labor approach to mutual problems? I suggest that he not only can; he should. Nothing, perhaps, was as telling for such a need as the report in mid-February 1985, by a Presidential Commission stating that the ability of American business to compete with other countries has been slipping for more than twenty years. Even in the high-technology field, the great hope of the American economy, there have been setbacks for seven of ten American industries.

The Commission urged closer cooperation among government, business, and labor. The panel, headed by John A. Young, president of the Hewlett-Packard Company, included businessmen, labor leaders, and others. "We encourage labor, management, and government to work toward a consensus on industrial issues," the report stated.

My own conviction is that if unions and management do form a cooperative alliance, a symbiotic relationship, it can be productive and profitable for all. Too often, profit is viewed in the abstract, a windfall for an elite group of Americans who manage and invest in business. But profit benefits the whole work force in ever expanding waves of employment, income, the ability to buy products and services, and the right to enjoy a fruitful life.

Profits are a by-product of efficiency and productivity, and both of these elements tend to decrease whenever the adversarial aspect of management-labor relations sharpens. That bitter relationship and the attitudes that build it represent a disease eating away at the heart of the collective bargaining process. The high rate of business bankruptcies, which recently reached a peak, reflects profits turned to losses. If companies are to provide jobs, they must remain profitable. If the bankruptcy rate is to be reduced, unions can no longer force management to operate at a loss. And management, too, cannot on the one hand behave dictatorially, spurning workers' needs, and on the other hand give in to labor merely to pass on high costs to the public.

Yet we have the ideologues who predictably declare for either management or labor as if the other doesn't matter. They do a disservice to both, merely fanning the flames of an adversarial relationship. None of these pundits seems to come up with a mutually beneficial program. They just go on, year after year, spouting the same tired formulae for discontent.

Unfortunately, many heads of companies and unions support this destructive game. The trouble is that management, facing a crisis, acts under pressure, often too late, while labor reacts, often too harshly.

I was recently contacted by a desperate employer facing a strike which developed from the long-brewing discontent of unionized workers. A week before the strike, I engaged in intensive strategy discussions with the owners. It was then that management decided to talk directly to the workers for the first time. But it was too late. The union members voted for the walkout because during the prior fifty-one weeks they had been ignored by management.

The strike was settled and the company gave the union more than it should have. Afterward, speaking about the head of the company, some of the workers told me, "We made him pay more than he should have because all that time he didn't treat us as human beings." But sadly enough, the owner didn't appear to have learned a thing. As soon as the strike was over, he bellowed to the workers over the public address system, "Now, let's get back to work!"

It was, needless to say, a message aimed to stimulate productivity. But it landed instead with a dull thud.

CHAPTER II

DO CONCESSIONS WORK?

"Negotiators are approaching contract talks in a retaliatory mood, with 'disdain for the employer and blood in their eye.' "

L ate in June, 1985, after an acrimonious 26-day hotel workers' strike, the first of its kind in New York city, 25,000 employees agreed to a new pact providing for wage increases of 23.5 percent in four increments over five years. The approximate annual wage gain of 4.5 percent, however, was carved out at quite a sacrifice. Because management bargained hard for wage stability, the New York Hotel & Motel Trades Council, which represents employees of 104 hotels, for the first time accepted a pact that did not include the possibility of a wage reopener or cost-of-living adjustment.

The union relaxed its usual insistance on rigid work rules and agreed to allow some employees to work at more than a single task. It also accepted a two-tier wage scale in which newly hired workers received less than longer-term employees. The union, whose members found the strike difficult to endure, hadn't wanted such a long lasting pact. It originally demanded an annual wage gain of 5.4 percent and wanted nothing to do with flexible work rules. The Association, however, had taken a tough stand in an effort to hold down costs as various cities increasingly competed for conventions and meetings. All in all, the union's concessions were a major victory for the Hotel Association of New York.

Nothing has so riled unions and encouraged management as the recent trend towards negotiated givebacks or concessions.

It has happened many times in the last decade and a half as companies girded to meet labor for contract renewal talks. "Not only won't there be any more money in the new contract," the management negotiator typically warned, "but we need a reduction in wages or fringes or changes in work-rules. Maybe all three. We won't make it through the year without it. We need concessions."

Givebacks when labor always wanted more? Employers asking for cuts instead of granting increases? Suddenly the push-pull process in labor talks was being reversed. Labor was being asked to surrender hard-fought gains it had won in earlier contracts talks, often after years of effort and strife. But was management being entirely sincere in its new demands? Could unions agree to promises that employees would be able to keep their jobs and that current union concessions would be returned later in good faith? If feelings were testy before, they became more bitter as unions began giving in to the irksome demands.

As more unions agreed to the givebacks in the late 1970s and early 1980s, their concessions resembled capitulation almost as if at the point of a gun. To management, the givebacks seemed a boon when they were most needed, the cavalry coming over the hill to the rescue. But neither side rested easy after they agreed to the difficult terms.

The background for the givebacks were the major strikes of the early 1980s and the highest jobless rate since the Depression. Labor concessions involving wage freezes, cost-of-living pay deferrals, or the elimination of paid holidays were something new and at the same time both disturbing and hopeful. They held the promise of a new, cooperative labor-management relationship. In a difficult economic time when sheer survival was at the heart of individual company negotiations, the willingness of unions to concede denoted a new attitude. It meant that workers were willing to sacrifice their own needs to help employers cut costs, compete, and survive.

But still there existed rigidity and abuses on both sides, as I found, and needed concessions were not always given. In Philadelphia, a few years ago, a group of stores operated by the Great Atlantic & Pacific Tea Company, otherwise known as A&P, urged the union to grant certain concessions in order to ensure the company's survival. The union adamantly refused. Later, the chain was forced to close many stores in the area. I happened to refer to that situation when I appeared on a Philadelphia television show. A labor leader in the audience spoke up to give labor's side of the story. "I would have given the concessions," he said. "Fine," I said, "but where were you when A&P needed them?" He shrugged. "At the time they asked for it," he replied, "we didn't think they needed concessions, especially after all the hard work the employees did."

But labor did grant givebacks to some large companies in recent years. In 1983, employees of Eastern Air Lines, the nation's third-largest air carrier, gave up a scheduled 18 percent wage increase and accepted a one-year wage freeze in return for 25 percent of Eastern's stock and four seats on its board of directors. That 1984 agreement was due to have its terms rescinded by year end and the union had been expecting that the wage freeze would be lifted.

But as Eastern prepared to submit a final estimate of its 1985 wage costs to its nervous creditors, Frank Borman, Eastern's board chairman, shocked his employees. He said that the wage freeze would be continued and that there would be no 18 percent wage increase. Because the company had been unprofitable since 1979, Eastern's chief said that it could not afford the additional $22 million per month in extra wages that the unions wanted. The announcement produced an uproar among Eastern's unions. Both sides sought help from the courts and the airline almost ran afoul of its lenders.

Up to that time, three other separate agreements involving concessions had drawn national attention. The Ford Motor Company was party to one in March, 1982. General Motors Corporation signed the second such agreement one month later. Both contracts dramatically illustrated labor's tortured decisions to grant major pay concessions in order to get a certain measure of job security. The two agreements involved a wage freeze for the contract's duration, a deferral of eighteen months in cost-of-living wage gains, and a reduction of paid holidays each year of the contract. In the third case, the Teamsters in its National Master Freight Agreement conceded a wage freeze, but in return obtained a portion of a cost-of-living adjustment provided in the previous contract.

What did both sides gain in these three cases?

The pact between GM and the Auto Workers Union was designed to save the big automaker up to $3 billion during the contract's term. As the price of settlement, GM rescinded its planned closing of four factories employing about eleven thousand workers and agreed to a two-year hold on further plant closings. GM also granted an income protection plan to longtime workers, instituted lifetime employment safeguards, and revised the financing of supplemental unemployment benefit funds.

Ford estimated that its agreement would save the company from $600 million to $1 billion. In exchange, the company agreed to a two-year moratorium on plant closings, an income provision for laid-off employees, and a job security program at two plants. Trucking companies also obtained substantial cost savings when they signed the master agreement with the Teamsters. The companies, however, agreed not to sell, lease, or transfer any part of their operations to third parties. They also agreed that laid-off workers would retain seniority throughout the life of the contract.

It was in the late 1970s that givebacks first made a major impact on the public. Teetering on bankruptcy, the Chrysler Corporation implored the United Auto Workers to accept a $1 billion cut in scheduled wage and fringe increases. Chrysler hoped that if it could win these concessions from the UAW, the company could get $1 billion-plus in Federal loan guarantees. But the demand threw the union in turmoil. In October, 1979 the membership agreed to defer the wage gains and to surrender paid personal holidays. This won the automaker some $446 million in loans. But Chrysler came back again for more union givebacks in order to obtain another $622 million in Federal loans.

The union became especially bitter over the second round of givebacks. Chrysler rallied and showed profits. The company, true to its word, started the profit-sharing plan for workers which it had promised in exchange for the concessions. But unfortunately, like the other auto producers, Chrysler continued to have large layoffs.

The givebacks, in other words, had not paid off for the union, while the benefit to the automaker was less than expected.

It was later, however, in the first quarter of 1982, that the rate of concessions increased sharply. In addition to the concessions which unions made in the GM, Ford, and Teamsters' agreements, eighty-eight other instances of concession bargaining were reported by the Bureau of National Affairs in that quarter.

The BNA stated:

An analysis of these 31 successfully concluded 'concession' negotiations showed that in slightly more than half, the union agreed to wage and benefit reductions (exclusive of holidays) while in slightly less than one-half the agreements, the unions agreed to a wage and benefit freeze. Unions agreed to give up paid holidays in almost 40 percent of the negotiated contracts and conceded to work-rule changes designed to improve productivity and reduce costs in slightly more than 40 percent of the contracts.

In exchange, employees received promises of future wage and benefit improvements in 25 percent of the concluded contracts contained in the database file. In more than one-third of the contracts, employees received either explicit or implicit promises of improvement in employment security.

The file also contains information on 36 situations in which negotiations over concessions were in progress in the first quarter of 1982. In addition, in 11 cases the union agreed to concessions, but the company or plant closed anyway, while in 13 cases negotiations were conducted after the plant shut down as the union attempted to secure a favorable severance pay agreement or an understanding on retirement or insurance for workers terminated by the shutdown.

That hectic period of union givebacks and desperate management demands was not to end without producing some disturbing results.

The GM-UAW pact was ratified in a close, 52 percent "for," 48 percent "against" vote. This slim margin indicated that union workers were reluctant to give up scheduled increases, even though they faced rapidly growing layoffs. The conviction grew that the concessions weren't always warranted. The United Parcel Service negotiations offer a case in point. UPS was highly profitable but wanted their employees to accept the same wage and benefit concessions as truckers who were part of the National Master Freight Agreement. A dissident group of Teamsters voted to fight ratification of the UPS pact. "We're going to see a lot of employers asking for concessions who don't really need them," observed John Zalusky, AFL-CIO economist.

Ironically, despite all the publicity and heat generated by givebacks, a former Secretary of Labor viewed them as relatively insignificant in influencing wage trends.

John T. Dunlop, a labor economist and Harvard professor, told a February 1982 Conference of Business economists, "While concession bargaining has come into play in situations where there has been a serious issue of economic survival, this type of bargaining will not significantly shape the level of dimensions of the 1982 general wage developments." He added that history has shown that "reductions in rules, fringes, or wage rates do not spread far from the particular enterprise or plant unless another company or plant confronts a similar threat to employment and survival and has been closely related in wage setting in the past."

Management Push vs. Labor Resistance

As a negotiator, I have found that confusion and confrontation inevitably seem to come in the wake of negotiated givebacks or stiff resistance to givebacks.

Consider, by way of example, the fresh-produce supplier in the Northeast whom I represented. He was having a very difficult time in his negotiations with the Teamsters' union. The company could not withstand a strike of more than a few days because of its perishable goods. The union, however, felt the pressure in other ways as well. Operating in a highly competitive industry, the company knew that if it couldn't serve its customers and its produce spoiled, rival companies would jump in. Talks with the president of the Teamsters' local proved useless. His position was simply that there was an industry-wide contract and nothing could be done specifically for that company.

The implication in this union squeeze play was that if the concern "couldn't cut the mustard," it would just have to go out of business. The union, however, didn't realize that this particular company wasn't going to take labor's tough stance lightly. The company seriously considered closing its business because the union's inflexible demands would make it noncompetitive with the rest of the market. It reminded me of what had happened to my own father's diaper business. In this case, however, the company's president became convinced that the company would be better off financially if it sold its assets and reinvested elsewhere. Why should it suffer the slow but certain economic death which would certainly result from giving in to the union's demands?

That particular incident highlights for me the reason unions have only reluctantly agreed to givebacks. Within the hierarchy of many unions there's the strong conviction that it has taken a long time to achieve a certain wage standard for an industry. Union leaders feel that by giving in to one company and creating a disparity in wages among several employers, the concessions that were won through hard, bitter struggle will begin to slip away and disappear. As a practical matter, the establishment of an industry standard has also made the union's role easier in collective bargaining. Union leaders could tell management, "This is what we've gotten from everybody else and we aren't going to take any less from you!"

There's one more reason for the reluctance to yield on concessions — political pressures within the union. The rank and file elect the officials, casting their ballots for those who have performed well on their behalf. If the officials permit concessions, they're afraid that some insurgent will suddenly appear, announce his candidacy, and run against the union leadership, claiming that the incumbent "sold out" the membership.

In my opinion, the combination of industry-wide contracts and internal union political pressures exerts a destructive viselike grip on collective bargaining. In practical terms, there shouldn't be automatic, nonnegotiable industry standards. Each company should rise or fall on its own ability to compete. That is the intrinsic nature of our economic system. Whether because they are more diversified, more efficient, or simply bigger, some companies manage to stay in business and compete at a given wage level much more efficiently than others. But efficiency by itself isn't always enough. The produce company might have been operating as efficiently as it could. But it didn't have the resources or the opportunity to become strong enough or large enough to compete with bigger firms.

In that case and probably many others, efficiency was hardly the factor that should determine whether or not industry rates should apply. The produce concern was just a small company trying to survive amid industry-wide standards which covered a broad spectrum of companies of all sizes. Unfortunately, an industry-wide standard imposes the greatest burden on the weaker, smaller companies. Automatically applying industry-wide wage standards to a particular company's problem, and at the same time excluding other economic approaches such as wage concessions, produces a peculiar irony for the labor unions as well as for an industry as a whole. Without the concessions, more than a few companies might well decide to have fewer jobs available for the union workers, the very ones who pay dues and contribute to a union's very survival.

In one sense, of course, givebacks are a means of getting out from under the burden of industry standards. The trucking industry provides an excellent example, and the situation there parallels many others. Givebacks became pronounced in the late 1970s as the recession began to steamroll. Major industries, including rubber, transportation, and trucking, obtained concessions. Concession fever then spread to other industries throughout the entire United States. By the time that the National Master Freight Agreement was renegotiated in the late 1970s, it became obvious that the Teamsters had been able to extract from the trucking industry just about everything it wanted. In earlier times labor had stretched to the limit the amount of wages and benefits that it could extract from the trucking industry. But deregulation of the trucking industry helped bring on a crisis. Nonunion companies entering the market with low overhead came into direct competition with companies saddled with the high wage rates and fringe benefits of the Teamsters' union contract. Basically, only the larger, unionized companies could grow because of their volume. But once the non-union truckers entered the picture, the business of many of the unionized carriers dried up, and that included some larger companies. Truckers fell like tenpins.

The union, however, grappling with its own political pressures and problems, often proved intransigent despite the obviously desperate situation of the industry.

The result, my own experience showed, had some complex results, often with tragic overtones. Take the example of a large trucking company in the East: In the early 1980s the firm found that it couldn't operate profitably for some of the reasons I mentioned above. The owners wanted to close the business. Doing so would have created some potentially serious legal and financial problems, such as a possible withdrawal liability to cover a multi-million dollar pension obligation. The owners therefore decided to sell the company to some members of management. These individuals agreed to buy, even though buying the company would entail assuming the pension liability. But they found themselves unable to raise sufficient funds. As a result, a condition of the sale was that the new owners would give existing employees the opportunity to buy preferred stock amounting to a limited interest in the new trucking company. The stock purchase would require about 85 percent of the employees to participate in order to get the company going. The union, however, resisted, probably because it feared that this new concept would weaken its ability to control the membership.

What followed was a comedy of errors and mutual misjudgment, a comedy that sadly put jobs, family fortunes, and company survival on the line.

Management decided to seek approval from the top of the Teamsters' hierarchy. The head of the state Teamsters' Conference objected after the company made an unsuccessful end run to the Eastern Conference of Teamsters for approval. The union asserted that the company was not only violating Federal labor law in bypassing the union's chain of command but was unilaterally implementing new terms in a contract. The union said that the company was, in effect, forcing employees to buy stock as a condition of employment. Technically, the Teamsters were right. But the pragmatic problem was the company's very life. If the company did not survive, it certainly would not be able to provide any jobs.

It was a classic case of confusion on each end. Management did not handle the situation properly. Just as importantly, the Teamsters' union simply wouldn't surrender any of its political control, wouldn't recommend that the employees go along, and in fact discouraged their participation. Yet slightly more than 50 percent of the workers did buy the stock. Unfortunately, it was far short of the amount needed to keep the company alive. It went out of business.

In fact, the inability of industry to obtain concessions was typical of what really happened throughout the country. For every industry or company which received concessions, there were others which received nothing from the union. The Teamsters have sometimes been a very recalcitrant union. Companies in the trucking industry, including many of our clients, sought concessions from that union to ease their difficulties. The Teamsters did not always agree to necessary concessions, and in some cases wouldn't even renegotiate new contracts. In this most difficult time for truckers, a good portion of them are still paying very high welfare, pension, and other benefits. Under the 1985 Master Freight Agreement, employers pay over $127.00 per employee per week for benefits. Internal political problems such as the 1983 fraud indictment and conviction of Roy Williams, the president of the International Brotherhood of Teamsters, have prevented any unanimous agreement in policy toward concessions. There has been nothing like the industry-wide concessions of auto, steel, and rubber.

One reason why the trucking industry has not granted broad concessions may be that labor is finding that controlling its own membership is a growing problem.

Take the case of a large commodity carrier in New Jersey. It found itself in a peculiar situation in 1983, a situation which gave the union leadership a case of severe heartburn. Employees in a section of the company doing local trucking wanted parity with those in another section doing long-haul trucking. The union's leadership termed the demand for parity "absolutely ridiculous" and said that there was no real basis for the demand. The employees involved went on strike for more than five months. The local-haul division practically closed down, due to depressed economic circumstances. The union, trying to cope with the demands of its members, could do nothing but take a stance opposing the company.

This is an aggravated case of labor's growing inability to keep the reins on its own members, which creates problems for negotiators on both sides. The Teamsters Union is an example of a union which has this problem because the rank and file increasingly oppose the union leadership. It is a large union which has become accustomed to getting increases, double-digit in size. It has also grown accustomed to a tough adversarial relationship with management. Perhaps because of the size and tough negotiating posture of the union, the Teamsters leadership has not been duly concerned with the impact that the obstinacy of its members had on business. When trucking companies asked for concessions, the union generally has not granted them because of the independence of the rank and file. In many cases, when the company has urged, "We need concessions," the union leadership has understood and sympathized but refused to go along because it knew it couldn't control the membership.

In general, many companies obtained concessions, but many more sought them without success. Unions were generally reluctant to grant them because doing so would have made a dent in industry-wide standards. Faced with unhappy members in a worsening economy, unions refused to make concessions because the leadership did not want to lose the support of the rank and file. The result has been confusion and a growing realization that givebacks haven't worked either for management or the workers. This, I believe, is the prime reason why the day of concessions is waning.

The national Union of Hospital and Health Care Employees, RWDSU, AFL-CIO, District 1199C, has adopted the motto, "No Givebacks." Its negotiators sit in management-labor meetings and proclaim, "No Givebacks." As I see it, givebacks are declining because they haven't yielded results.

The Looming Confrontation over Givebacks

There are two principal reasons why a confrontation will erupt over givebacks.

Workers agreed to givebacks on salary gains, benefits, paid holidays, and other provisions because the struggling economy threatened to take away their jobs. The growing sentiment among workers is that, at the first opportunity, they will not only want to recoup what they gave up but also make some new gains.

This demand will be reinforced because many promises management made as a price for the concessions haven't been forthcoming. In some cases, the savings weren't applied to remodel plants in order to increase jobs or make them more productive. In others, workers were dismayed to find that the business pickup did not bring more job security or more jobs. As a result, the awareness that the givebacks were all just some sort of put-on, a rip-off, has been growing among the ranks of unionized labor. That is the assessment of William Wynn, president of the 1 million member United Food and Commercial Workers International Union (UFCW). According to him, employers demanding concessions often allowed their greed to exceed their need and in the process destroyed their credibility. Many UFCW negotiators are therefore approaching contract talks in a retaliatory mood, "with disdain for the employer and a certain amount of blood in their eye." The disappointments and frustrations of concession bargaining will surely intensify as the economy continues to improve and industry moves to capitalize on the brighter business climate.

Add to that the growing perception that givebacks simply have not worked. Despite all the hullabaloo and the wrenching on the union side, companies are beginning to find that the givebacks weren't enough. Look at Eastern Air Lines' situation, where the concessions in the 1984 contract not only didn't help enough to permit the promised recoupment in the 1985 contract but failed to prevent a near impasse with the corporate lenders as well. In both the oil and steel industries, the percentage of labor costs given back wasn't nearly enough to make much difference. The steel industry neither became more competitive worldwide nor sufficiently competitive in the domestic market. This is also true of the oil industry.

So what are both sides telling themselves after all the push-and-pull of concessions? Business is saying, "Yes, it's true that we got something back after all those years of giving, but it wasn't enough to make a real difference." Workers are saying, "Now that you're finally making a profit again, give us back what we gave you and something else, too." But business isn't going to oblige with givebacks-plus-interest and labor isn't going to take less. The results of this are obvious.

Why didn't the concessions work?

The apparently large giveback in the steel industry was actually only a deferral; not really a giveback, it was a sort of tax shelter in which ultimate payment was only delayed. And even with this deferment of cost which could be transferred into improved productivity, the likelihood of creating new jobs is faint. That reinvestment of capital has gone and will increasingly go toward installing new, modern equipment which will be operated largely by robots. The goal in the steel industry, as in the auto industry, is the highest possible degree of automation in order to provide enhanced competitive clout. So one big reason givebacks haven't worked is that technology is at war with high employment, so the concessions aren't going to change that much at all. It doesn't seem to matter that plowing the cost savings back into local plants to build jobs was part of the givebacks agreement. Pragmatism took over, but workers will see that only as a rip-off.

The same squeeze play with unhappy results has also occurred in the nonunion sector of the U.S. economy. There, despite the lack of media coverage, givebacks have been even more prevalent than in the organized sector. In both sectors, I have seen cases where companies ought not to have asked for concessions but did so anyway. And that will certainly heat up the situation. What will probably develop in the nonunion field, as workers find that they aren't getting back the concessions they made, will be a new organizational effort by unions to stake out claims in what has been fallow territory. Organized labor will probably be more successful, too, as nonunion workers find themselves frustrated but unable to express their frustration except through the formal means of unionization.

There is another element in the picture, which, I believe, adds a further, disturbing dimension. As the confrontation approaches, the public will find itself upset and frustrated over the converging, increasingly antagonistic forces of management and labor. The public anger is worrisome because it can only add to the likelihood of confrontation and possibly violence.

The public certainly showed its resentment during the transit strikes in Philadelphia and New York in the early 1980s. When interviewed by reporters, many commuters expressed anger over the discomfort and delays they faced during the stoppages. It was the sort of resentment that erupts when everything seems to go wrong.

Consider the SEPTA strike in the early 1980s in the Greater Delaware Valley, the area which embraces Philadelphia and its suburban towns. This was a strike that crippled a major transportation system and turned many people against unionism. In order to stay alive, SEPTA's five-county regional, rail-commuter division was compelled to imitate private industry by laying off workers and consolidating job classifications. This aroused the union's resentment, so the union moved to protect jobs, regardless of the company's problems. The strike was mild and unsuccessful on the first day. That changed the second day because of violent mass picketing. The general discomfort and dislocation didn't seem to bother many commuters for the first few days, but soon after, the inconvenience and time lost annoyed them seriously. It didn't matter whether this was a public or private sector strike. What did matter was the public inconvenience that results when a public service is no longer available. The public reacted in the same way when President Reagan decided that enough was enough and fired the striking air traffic controllers. People felt that the striking union had no right to inconvenience the whole nation just to serve the interest of a small group of people. Similarly, the six-week-strike in 1983 of the Metro North line in the New York area left many riders unhappy and publicly proclaiming that they would no longer use the line when it resumed operations. Both the union and management lost in that strike.

The public also loses when teachers strike. Unfortunately, teacher walkouts have become as much a part of the fall season as the World Series. When teachers strike, children of both labor and management families suffer and the educational system weakens. Against a background of continual strikes, the public now dwells not on what the teachers are demanding nor on what the school boards say they can give, but on the turmoil that the strikes create for the public.

It's especially disconcerting to me to realize that, whether strikers may have just cause or not, the public's patience is shorter in a period of difficult economic conditions. Violence can't be far away when that occurs. Whether a business-labor confrontation arises over the matter of givebacks or for any other cause, it is hard to predict the public's temper. But it will hardly be sweet and forbearing.

Can the Confrontation Be Avoided?

The need for a new, more wholesome climate in management-labor relations is certainly vital. One cannot help feeling a sense of urgency about it. Management and labor must set aside their internal and external political considerations. Management must become more cooperative, more giving, and more informative in helping unions to understand what the real problems are. And labor, in turn, must cope with the responsibility of softening its normal adversarial attitude and join with management to improve productivity. Labor must consider assisting not only its members but also the company. Unions must overcome their archaic tendency towards rigid job classifications. The rigidity of unions compels management to become inflexible, produces inefficiency, and cuts down productivity.

The essence of avoiding confrontation may well hinge on timing. But the focus on timing must not become an obstacle to an organized, disciplined program of working for mutual benefit. Yet as the current scenario progresses in its ponderous, painful way toward a series of confrontations and possibly a violent denouement, it might be opportune to get back to some bedrock thinking. "When things aren't going right," growled Vince Lombardi, the legendary coach of the Green Bay Packers, "it's time to get back to the basics."

That may appear more simplistic than it really is. It's clear that somewhere within the relationship of management and labor, the fundamentals, the real objectives, the key issues, have been overcome by the heat, the passion, and the politics on each side. The solution, simplistic or not, is to start over, scrap the old shibboleths and prejudices, and unearth those forgotten basics. It will be a prime goal of this book to spell out those basics, the means and tools of a new approach. Givebacks are only one of the problems, albeit the most publicized. Together with the strikes of recent years, givebacks have been the most dramatic example of how the opponents have tried to best one another, circling around one another fearfully and nervously, yet failing to reconcile their differences.

By company and by industry, millions of workers must be convinced that they are part of the decision-making process. If so, they will understand the problems of industry to a much greater degree than they do now. They will accept the good with the bad and not feel that castor oil is being forced down their throats. Involvement in decision-making should include not only unionized but nonunionized workers, too, who are generally in the same boat regarding givebacks, layoffs, and job security.

The distance between management and labor in many American companies has often been more like an unbridgable chasm than a gap. Both sides have tried to maximize their own benefits and have seen the other side as an obstacle to that goal. How then will it be possible to involve workers in the decisions of management in such a way that the final decisions will benefit the entire company, both workers and management?

Perhaps the best way to arrive at a framework for worker-involvement is through a series of questions which might aptly be raised on the matter.

Question—*We appear to be in the middle of a short-term problem, but you are asking for a broad overview to correct it. Is there one way it can be achieved, a shortcut?*

Answer—It's difficult because of the adversarial mentality that both management and labor have exhibited over the last two decades. Let's take a basic issue that is certain to arise if both sides agree. Unions will inevitably ask, "Let's see your financial problem by looking at your figures." Obviously, one cannot suggest that payroll records be turned over for union study so that all salaries, including those of executives, are revealed and every expense account is listed. But the union and its members, if we expect them to cooperate in a new environment, will expect to see reliable data on which they, too, can base decisions. Giving the union this sort of information will cut through a lot of doubt and suspicion.

Question—*Will many businessmen show financial statements to a union?*

Answer—Yes, they will—and they should when there is a legitimate loss and the businessman is asking the union to recognize it and give him a concession to reduce it. The union has a legal right in many situations to that information anyway. It's vital to establish credibility in concession bargaining. I have been involved in many concession situations in the past several years, and the first thing that I have found essential is that management must offer the financial data to the union and give it a chance to audit the data if that is what the union desires. And I have found that where the company does it, the chances for successful bargaining are improved.

Question—*What about joint management-labor committees which are set up to bring both sides closer? Aren't they working?*

Answer—They aren't utilized enough. As an example, there's a New Jersey association of automobile dealers which has set up a management-labor committee to establish an apprenticeship program. New entry-level workers in the program can learn to be mechanics. In effect, the union is allowing the employer to develop a pool of trainee mechanics who won't get, say, $9.00 an hour right off the bat but who will start at, say, $3.50 an hour. Eventually the trainee comes up to the $9.00 an hour rate, but it might take a few years. The employer is deriving the benefit of later having qualified mechanics but training them at less than the full rate. The union has the benefit of replenishing its ranks, inviting new blood. Unfortunately, despite the fact that the concept exists and is provided for in the contract, neither management nor labor is working at it, at least not in the manner to make it succeed. There's apathy in that situation. It's tantamount to both sides saying, "Let's wait until the problem reaches a crisis state and then we'll deal with it." That type of muddled thinking must change.

Question—*Let's be really candid now. Aren't businessmen being downright unrealistic to expect a union rank and file worker to agree to eliminate his job category, to eliminate his job?*

Answer—Of course, it's difficult. But I think that in certain situations there is no choice. If a company in trouble finds no cooperation across the table, it has only a few options, all of them difficult. Major steel companies are going out of that industry and entering other fields. Eventually we may not have a steel industry in the United States, and where will that leave us but at the mercy of foreign producers. Companies are just packing up and moving to other areas and turning nonunion. For the worker to hang tough to preserve his job when the entire company may disappear is ridiculous. It's going to defeat the very thing he and his union are trying to accomplish—to save jobs.

Question— *That brings us back full circle to givebacks. So have they been just a disappointment and a failure?*

Answer— They sometimes add to the adversarial climate and should be avoided, if possible. The implication of asking for and granting concessions is that it involves the company's survival, but that hasn't been so in many cases. Yet there is something which is even more paramount than solely taking back from employees what they have earned in the past. I'm referring to keeping jobs. Givebacks have only been a patent remedy. What is really needed is a prescription resulting from a thorough professional examination. There must be, in effect, a meeting of the minds of both sides in the interest of mutual benefit. We might frame the problem this way: Does an employee of a trucking company want to be the highest-paid unemployed truck driver? Or does he want to continue working and earn a fair wage? There can be, of course, only one sensible answer. But the employee is likely to give that answer only if his employer deals with him openly and honestly.

CHAPTER III

BRAWLERS WITH BLINDERS

"Don't worry. We'll get your jobs back. We'll force the company to reopen."

E arly 1985, when management and labor had already traded bloody blows over a lengthy period, seemed right for some much needed enlightenment. The hard winter was almost at an end. The economy had improved and the tired opponents across the negotiating table might reasonably have taken a new tack. At first it looked as if the old confrontational pattern was about to change. Labor experts initially took heart and spirits rose. But within days, they fell.

A Fantasy Revived

It was February 28. At the professional baseball owners' meeting in Fort Lauderdale, Lee MacPhail, the owners' top negotiator, took the unusual step of asking the players' negotiators for their help in solving the game's growing economic problems. Conceded MacPhail, "They're [the players' agents] going to have to see some financial records anyway to see what we're talking about. We're concerned about the welfare of the game, the financial structure of the game. We asked them to sit down together with us and work out joint solutions."

The players' response came from Donald Feir, acting executive director of the Players Association. He told MacPhail that if the owners thought they had a financial problem and could prove it: "We will consider it. Tell us what you're thinking of and what you want us to do with some specifics. Then we'll be able to respond."

In baseball, that dialogue was unusual. It was also promising, as it would be anywhere else in the American economy. The message — "let's talk; we'll show you the books; let's work together" — seemed a bright ray of sunlight in a murky world.

But in the airline industry on that very day, it was, instead, the same old, tired impasse ending in a strike. Pan American World Airways had just won a concession from its pilots' union to stretch out deferred raises of 25.7 percent over the thirty-two month length of the contract. But unlike the Air Line Pilots Association, the Transport Workers Union was disinclined to go along with the airline's pleas that it was unable to pay more than a 20 percent wage hike over three years. Pan Am hadn't made a profit since 1980.

The company's position was supported by a study of Pan Am by Lazard Freres and Company, the investment bankers. Pan Am's board of directors ordered the study which found that Pan Am couldn't afford to pay the full wage increases already deferred since 1981. But the study also reproached the airline by adding that "the unwillingness to confront Pan Am's employees with the full consequences of the airline's condition had contributed significantly to the current difficulties." The next day, the TWU went out on strike.

So it was back again to the same old slugging match. For many decades management and labor have warily circled one another, much like tired heavyweights in a boxing ring. First one side looped a punch, then the other, and soon blood spattered the canvas. It has been a long, unending series of threats, confrontations, litigation, strikes, and even violence. Because of faulty, misguided objectives, the weary exercise has wasted time and opportunity.

The history of American labor relations, in fact, is studded with examples of shockingly bad judgment on both sides, along with greed, hypocrisy, and counterproductive, self-serving demands. But nothing has been more disappointing, more frustrating, than what has rankled at the core of the employer-union relationship in the last decade and a half; namely, a long-ingrained conviction that one side *must* win and the other *must* lose. The result has been long years of resentment and brooding, long years of lost possibilities for harmony. The luster of good economic times alone hid the poison. But the true feelings have erupted to the surface during bad times.

In the thirty-year sweep of industrial productivity, growth, and national prosperity which lasted from the end of World War II in 1945 through the mid-1970s, the United States lulled itself into a euphoric fantasy. Employers convinced themselves that rising labor costs could largely be passed on to consumers. As long as their profit margins continued to rise, partly because business could pass on higher costs to the consumer, employers were not overly concerned by the rapidly increasing costs of labor. The public, too for the most part, was quite willing to absorb the higher price tags in the marketplace. Why not? Inflation was high, but it seemed to be growing only moderately in the first quarter century after the war. It wasn't until the next decade, when consumers read and heard that the percentage increases in the prices of goods and services had soared to a double-digit level, that they began to balk.

Everyone was fooled by the favorable ratio of supply and demand. As long as product orders and backlogs were high, management was reluctant to face the interruption of a strike. For years management persisted in the conviction that the assembly lines had to keep humming at all costs. The conviction came naturally, perhaps, during the 1950s and 1960s when management, labor, and the public felt little concern about foreign competition. In the automotive field, the domestic manufacturers virtually had a monopoly on the market. This was also generally true of other large industries, such as steel, rubber, transportation, aircraft manufacturing, and airlines. As the gross national product grew and corporate profits mounted, unions and their members insisted on a larger share of the pie. Didn't they, after all, deserve it, considering the importance of their contribution? Management very often said yes, and agreed to exorbitant increases again and again.

This attitude of workers that they could always extract more and of management that it could pass on the costs eventually resulted in this montage of problems:

 * Employee and union demands became outrageous.

* Management often capitulated, sometimes to the point of foolishness.
* Higher and higher levels of employee expectations reinforced the prevalent attitude that "if we got what we wanted in the past, why can't we get what we want now?"
* Employers were more concerned with increasing their market share by competing with each other rather than with the growing influx of imports.
* Wages escalated sharply but productivity did not keep pace.
* In the 1960s particularly, labor pushed for even more fringe benefits. Along with other union leaders, Lane Kirkland of the AFL-CIO and Douglas Fraser of the UAW talked of a four-day workweek, more days off, more sick-leave time, and more vacations.
* As the yearning for more leisure time grew among Americans, they became more conspicuous in their consumption, buying more imported goods with little or no concern as to how that might ultimately affect their own livelihood.
* All of this generated the perception in America — and particularly in the American workplace — that we were riding a happy wave that would never, could never, ebb.

The frightening aspect of this dark scenario was that it resembled the same 1920s fantasy and mindless bubble which created the decade-long Great Depression of the 1930s.

There is no doubt that a distinct parallel exists between the present situation and that of the 1920s and 1930s. Is it possible that the seeds of disaster created by the greed and self-interest on both sides of the bargaining table sprouted in the decade beginning in the mid-1970s and led to the worst recession in many years? If the United States is currently digging itself out of that economic morass, a bit of introspection is certainly in order. Unless we remember the mistakes and misjudgments of the recent past, the next economic downturn may be even worse, perhaps irreversible. At the least, we could certainly go the way of Great Britain, slipping, sliding, plunging into economic vegetation. At the worst . . . who knows?

These hypothetical possibilities aside, the confusion which

inevitably emerged from bargaining at cross-purposes only served to arouse bitterness and frustration.

While management was in the *giving* mood and labor was in the *taking* mood, business refused to rock the boat and imperil the trend of rising profits.

Yet, despite the easy give and the easy take, many workers began to feel a growing sense of dehumanization. They were simply pawns in the marketplace, taken for granted as much as the plant's equipment. Concepts such as the Japanese system of quality circles or even basic techniques of communication were never seriously employed by management in the 1960s and early 1970s. Management became increasingly stratified. The middle management layer, including plant supervisors, and the workers began to detest each other as well as senior management.

In fact, what seemed to be developing were separate worlds in which the occupants cared less and less about those in the contiguous world and more and more about their own wants and needs. The so-called "company team," the pride of industrial America, was crumbling. Workers were convinced that they were really not part of that team and that the company did not really care about them. The irony of it may have been that the demands of employees for excessive increases in wages and fringes actually represented the workers' craving for recognition. In other words, if they weren't to get a "thank you" or a pat on the back or some other indication that they "belonged," the push for more dollars provided the only reasonable alternative.

But my experience shows that, in reality, the reverse can often be the case.

If employees are treated fairly, I have found, and are recognized for performing well, even with such a hackneyed phrase as "Thank you for a job well done," they will generally ask for fewer dollars in new contracts. The only qualifier to this is whether or not the employees believe they are being paid fairly. It is, of course, difficult to define what "fairly" means to employees or to the employers. But I have found that it is generally easier to work out a "fair" contract settlement when employees believe that they are not being taken for granted. It is generally the petty issues which constitute "unfair" treatment and which normally bog down the negotiating process, leading either to strikes or to contracts with excessive wage increases, signed only to avoid or end strikes.

Some solutions must be found to eradicate labor's craving for a "pound of flesh" from management.

My approach is a basic one. The "pound of flesh" attitude will remain unless we involve our employees more intimately in the policy-making decisions of the company. The attitudes of American workers must change, but they can only change if American management takes greater initiative in recognizing their efforts and casts off at least some of its inhibitions that have proven so self-defeating.

While some employers are recognizing the importance of having a better relationship with their employees, too many employers still relegate labor relations to a secondary role. Too many employers are still convinced that if they communicate more openly with their workers and allow them a role in making decisions, they will be abrogating their own responsibilities. This refusal to communicate openly is actually a paralysis of fear. It brings to mind the tortoise who never emerges from his shell. And he gets nowhere, nowhere at all.

The real nub of the problem is that American management too often responds only to crisis. Suddenly, when the fearsome scythe is swinging, employers talk one-to-one to employees. "Look now," the boss is telling them in effect, "things are damned rough right now. You've got to pitch in, tighten your belt, take some food away from your wife and kids, and help us out of this spot." That, of course, gets the expected and deserved reaction. Because communications with workers are neither constant nor regular, employees tend to be skeptical whenever management does respond to them in an open way. That is especially true in a crisis when employees clearly understand that management is opening up only because it is under the gun and it wants something from them. The fact of the matter is that if management only talks when the pressure is on, employees are probably right in not responding.

An incident that I experienced shows that management sometimes conjures up fears that are way out of proportion with what really happens when an employer does communicate with those who work for him.

On a recent occasion I told an employer that he ought to involve his employees in some elements of the decision-making process. I suggested the use of a questionnaire to facilitate the process. "I can't do that," he said.

"Why?"

He didn't respond immediately and I went on, "Do you feel that your employees may tell you how they feel and you may not like it?"

Reluctantly he conceded. I told him to try to determine what his employees thought about their current benefits and holidays, just for starters. But again he demurred. "That could give me some problems," he said.

"What kind of problems?"

"What will I do if I can't afford to give them the holidays or additional benefits they might want?" he asked.

"Just tell them you can't afford it."

As he pondered that, I added, "It's better to tell them the truth on a regular basis than to wait to do it at the bargaining table or when there is already a standoff. There's something else, too. Even if you can't afford the holidays or benefit increases, at least you will know how they feel and what their perceptions are."

He agreed to a questionnaire. Then I asked the employer to make two lists on a sheet of paper. One list would show how much the company was willing to give the employees in wage and benefit increases. The other list would contain what he anticipated they would ask for on such matters as hours, wages, and benefits. He did that while waiting for the questionnaires to be returned. When the returns were tallied and compared with his expectations, he found that the employees had asked for 20 percent less than he had predicted. The employer then gave them what they wanted, came out a hero, and at the same time saved money.

How the Stage Was Set for Tough Bargaining

It was natural that the fantasy and paranoia which gripped both sides of the bargaining table for the last fifteen years or so could only lead to greater confrontations. The framework for the confrontations had been bolstered not only by the mutual fears of labor and management but also by their perceptions of each other. Labor saw management as greedy but not strong enough to stand up for its own convictions. Employers viewed labor as too demanding and ridden with the rifts of internal politics. Those perceptions were accurate as far as they went.

Labor sought more and added different types of demands during the negotiating process. The union hierarchy found itself forced to constantly seek greater contract improvements than in the past in order to be reelected. But as the economy eroded and job security, rigid job classification, and more protection of employee rights came under new pressure, management found its prerogatives limited. Unions pressed forward if for no other reason than to reaffirm their very existence. This, of course, was complicated by the increasing intrusion of Federal legislation into all aspects of labor law and labor relations. That influence began to spread because of the Equal Employment Opportunity Act, the improvements in the Federal minimum wage, and laws that protected employees against discrimination because of age and disabilities. Even employees handicapped by alcoholism and drug addiction found themselves protected by Federal law.

All this became the backdrop for the very tough negotiations that started in the 1970s, crept into the 1980s, and led in desperation to the demands of management for givebacks in the early 1980s.

In the 1970s, unions weren't listening closely to the employers' claims that they could not both give in to heavy demands and stay in business. The trucking industry's national freight negotiations with the Teamsters union are a good example of this. The bargaining was complicated by the fact that employers historically told employees that they couldn't afford the new contract demands. Management negotiators didn't anticipate that, after a while, a big credibility gap would develop. Reluctance to reveal financial information to the unions only confounded matters. Thus, cries by management that it couldn't pay and couldn't afford the demands went unheeded by labor. All this was further complicated by labor's lack of responsibility or unwillingness to soften the demands of its insurgent rank and file.

As I sat at the bargaining table during the 1970s, I often heard union officials say that the cost of bread and milk was going up. Inflation had gone double-digit, they complained, and that was reason enough for their hard bargaining stance. So the unions were demanding not only double-digit increases but even heftier increases to cover what they feared would be a continuing rise in the cost of living. Ironically, this sort of thing only contributed to more inflation.

As the 1980s dawned, it was already clear that the U.S. was in a severe economic downturn as shown by a drop in GNP and business activity, rising unemployment, and a sharply higher rate of bankruptcies. Labor tried to exploit its old strength, the utilization of the political process which had been so successful under President Jimmy Carter. He had appointed to the National Labor Relations Board several people sympathetic to labor unions. Labor was confident that it could regain some strength from these appointments, and it was right. The NLRB began to render more pro-union and pro-employee decisions.

The Carter-appointed Labor Board established several prohibitions against companies shutting down their plants and running away, even if the companies were *shutting* and *running* to survive. The NLRB looked into every aspect of a plant closure. If it found even a remote indication of antiunion *animus*, it increasingly took the position that the closing or relocation represented a runaway shop. As punishment when it found that the employer did close and relocate for antiunion reasons, the agency ordered that the plant be reopened. Employers resisted. For the most part, they had only resorted to relocation when they were convinced that there was a sound, economic advantage to it. But labor largely failed in its effort to reverse this process through political clout. This was because employers who were ordered to reopen their plants in union territory reacted by taking the bankruptcy route or by making some sort of settlement with only back pay or by staging only a limited reopening. The punitive action, in other words, didn't produce the desired results but just added salt to the wound in the management-labor relationship. The result was fewer jobs in the area.

Moreover, the political muscle which unions tried to apply through the NLRB often threw impediments in the collective bargaining mechanism. I heard union officials assert many times, in negotiating sessions, "You can't close, and if you do, we'll file unfair labor charges against you." So the adversarial pressure was just intensified at a time when management and labor should have been working out their differences sincerely so that the plants could reopen and jobs be retained.

In fact, because of this type of squeeze play, the rate of factory migration had already soared to record levels during the 1970s. The economic prosperity of a number of southern states, particularly North Carolina and Georgia, rose dramatically as a result. Characteristically, labor responded both too late and too little to the growing threat. Labor did not want to grant concessions. That led to twin body blows to unionism. First, unions learned to their distress that companies weren't bluffing when they insisted that they were either moving or going out of business. Second, when businesses closed despite union promises to members that the companies were bluffing, the employees grew more cynical toward their leaders. It was as though the union ranks had been sold down the river twice, and their reaction was bitter. Insurgents rose to contest the union leadership.

That internal battling was behind the 1982 referendum among General Motors' unionized workers on the issue of concessions. A stunning 48 percent voted against the givebacks. This was obviously a new militancy at work within the union itself, not only against management but against union leaders as well.

While seated at the bargaining table recently, I began to hear for the first time recognition and admission that labor had demanded and wrested too much from management during the so-called "good times" of the 1960s and 1970s. It was clearly an expression of growing cynicism against the labor chiefs.

Not too long ago my colleagues and I were in the midst of contract negotiations with the Teamsters on behalf of a national paint producer in the East who had closed a plant in that area and relocated because of excessive union demands. During many contract talks in which the company threatened to close the plant, the union continued to promise its members that the closure wouldn't take place. Even after the plant was closed and employees were laid off, the union persisted in the charade. "Don't worry," union members were told, "we'll get your jobs back. We'll force the company to reopen." The union hierarchy kept insisting on this, despite the fact that it was shown evidence by the company that it would cost millions of dollars more to operate in the state it had departed than at other locations. The sad irony of all this is that the union membership believed its leaders not only at first but even after the plant moved.

Yet, in all this, the union leaders' position was that their very presence had been helpful and protective for the workers. If they weren't around, the union chiefs claimed, more plants would close and more in the way of givebacks would be captured by employers. But, as this incident showed, the truth is that too often the rigidity of unions has only been self-defeating. There are a number of instances in almost every industry in which unions took a tough position, forcing a company to close facilities and eliminate jobs. There are also cases where the union assisted the company to keep the plant open or to remain in operation. Unhappily, the jobless ranks are filled with more of the highest-paid union truck drivers, steel workers, and auto employees than ever before.

For that reason and others, labor today is fighting for its life. The image of labor unions as the champions of working people has been tarnished because some of the top officials have been indicted or are on the verge of indictment for criminal activity. Membership is at an all-time low. Both on a national and local level, union leaders fear that if elections were held tomorrow, they would not be returned to office. Unionism, in fact, faces a disturbing dilemma. If labor continues to capitulate, its leadership will be viewed by the rank and file as impotent and in need of replacement. But if the leadership doesn't capitulate with the many companies that remain on the economic brink, it will lose more and more members.

To what does it all point?

The solution of the dilemma is similar to what we recommended earlier to management. Within labor, some open, honest dialogue is necessary in contrast to rabble-rousing or blue-sky boasting. Labor, in short, needs to involve its own rank and file in more honest decision-making. Union members must be informed why employers are asking for givebacks, what economic conditions cause the employer's problems, and why getting a "pound of flesh" from the employer now will not amount to much later on. As with management, labor's attitude toward its own members must change.

If labor leaders told their members why a forthright management-union dialogue was necessary and also communicated openly and regularly with the rank and file, it's quite possible that more amicable contracts could be worked out without labor strife. It's certainly reasonable for labor to advise its constituents that one of the keystones for the 1980s and 1990s is the preservation of jobs. Job preservation is reasonable, all right, but it cannot be sought at all costs. Job security can't be a guarantee. It cannot be pushed through at the point of endless demands. But it may be obtained through the joint cooperation of both management and labor. Achieving job security will require work, lots of it.

Now the rallying cry in labor is obtaining job security at all costs, including making givebacks contingent on job protection. That may bring the same problem of undue pressure that will ultimately close plants and eliminate jobs. A Teamsters' official told me recently that the union will approve concessions if management provides automatic job security for three years for all employees and posts a bond to that effect. The response of the president of the company to that offer was: "I can't give that guarantee because I don't know if I'll be alive tomorrow."

Thus, some of the problems which have been forced on the bargaining negotiations of the 1980s, despite the adjustment in the national economy, have occured only because of the unbending, unrealistic attitudes exhibited by both sides.

CHAPTER IV

GOVERNMENT AND LABOR: AN INTERNATIONAL SCORECARD

"As a result, during the past two decades of rapid growth, the Japanese auto industry has been untroubled by the long strikes that were regular events in Detroit in the 1970s."

Who sets policy for and implements American labor relations? You might be surprised, even dismayed, to learn the answer.

Most often the public gives too much credence to the upper echelon officials in government for their influence on labor policy enforcement. We view the Secretary of Labor, the Chairman of the National Labor Relations Board, even the Secretary of Commerce, as the arbiters of what management and unions carve out at the bargaining table. And we assume that when either a Republican or Democratic administration comes into power, government policy will swing pro-employer or pro-labor.

The difficulty with this misconception is that it contains a particle of truth, even though it is mostly erroneous.

As I have learned over the years, the people who really control labor relations are the frontline and middle-level bureaucrats, the professional government executives who remain in their jobs regardless of the ebb and flow of administrations. More than a few of the field examiners whom I have met at the National Labor Relations Board, the Equal Employment Opportunity Commission, or the Federal Mediation and Conciliation Service entered the government because of its security, its substantial time off and its excellent pension benefits. The sad fact is that many of the very bright people who start in Federal service find their upward mobility slow and frustrating and their personal drives hampered. As a result many of them channel their ambitions into private industry or private practice. Many others, who remain, are resigned to their fate or frustrations, or are satisfied despite the limitations of their jobs.

In my opinion the exodus of many of the highly ambitious, achievement-oriented people has an effect on the government careerist. Many bureaucrats whom I've encountered and who either move up or remain in their posts for years seem to develop a certain antipathy toward the businessman or private practitioner.

When I started working for the NLRB about twenty years ago, I was an idealistic law school graduate who thought that our country's labor policies were applied equally, fairly, and objectively. I wanted to be one of those government people who made a major contribution to society by being recognized as fair and hardworking. But what I found around me put a damper on my idealism. The NLRB, it seemed to me, favored labor and did not remain neutral when it adjudicated unfair labor practice cases.

On one of my early days I attended a meeting to determine whether a complaint should be issued against an employer. One of the staff members made a comment which struck me as an attempt at humor but which I didn't find funny. Referring to the businessman and his associates named in the complaint, this long-time government official said, "It's not a question of who's telling the truth but who's lying the least." The clear implication, of course, was that neither employers nor union representatives could be believed.

There was also an underlying consideration in the issue of deciding whether or not the government would prosecute or otherwise litigate against the employer. It seemed to me that it was not so much the legal issues involved which mattered but how the employees could be helped after being allegedly discharged because of their union activities. After some discussion it was decided that the considerations on each side virtually offset each other. But since there were some credibility questions regarding how the employer had behaved, it was decided that a complaint should be issued because it would probably put pressure on him to settle the matter. The amount of back wages involved probably didn't total more than $15,000 to $20,000. But the thinking was that if a trial ensued, the employer's legal fees to defend that type of case would probably exceed $20,000.

The rationale expressed by some at the meeting was that the employer would settle on the basis that it was the better business decision for him to do so. It didn't matter that he was being discriminated against or that the legal issues weren't being properly addressed. It was the sort of thinking which has at times been characteristic of the way the government behaves when it is called upon to judge management-labor disputes.

It seemed to me that some people at the meeting were presuming the employer guilty and that unless he promptly established his innocence, a complaint would be issued against him. It seemed to me then as it does now that the more appropriate solution when legal and factual questions exist is to proceed with further, unbiased investigation. This is certainly preferable to taking the easy route of issuing a complaint and then compelling the employer to prove his innocence before an administrative law judge at an NLRB hearing.

But there was another disturbing dimension to the decision reached at that particular NLRB meeting. The decision seemed to rest on the premise that it was easier for an employer to pay $20,000 for back wages to employees than it would be for employees to lose those wages. It would have been, in fact, a greater hardship for the employees than for the employer, but this circumstance hardly justified the decision. The NLRB seldom realizes that by being overly protective of labor, workers in our society develop an attitude that they can do whatever they want and demand whatever they want. Workers come to think that the employer's hands are tied and that if an employer tries to tamper with employees' rights, they can run to the NLRB, complain loudly, and be protected.

So much for that incident, an incident which most likely has been repeated many times under many different circumstances. But in any widespread situation where excesses continue unchecked for a long period, both irony and redress inevitably arise.

For years labor enjoyed the power of the Board to protect it and to control employer rights. The NLRB prosecutes employers much more frequently than unions. This is so despite the fact that amendments to the Taft-Hartley Act balanced, at least legislatively, the scale which weighs unfair labor practices on either side.

On the other hand, more recently things have begun to change. I don't want to suggest it is a dramatic change, but there definitely has been a move in a different direction. For example, in a relatively recent case decided by the U.S. Supreme Court, labor unions were informed that they could be prosecuted for failing to represent employees properly and that they could be held accountable and have to pay back wages to union members for breach of that duty. It was an interesting development, but it isn't certain where it will go. It's likely that such cases will be the exception rather than the rule. Judging by past actions of the Board's investigators, I feel strongly that they will more likely than not fail to take the initiative to prosecute the unions.

This was certainly dramatized in a case which occurred in an eastern region of the NLRB. It involved a company distributing and warehousing food items for schools and institutional facilities. Three years ago the company was shut down by a long, violent strike called by a Teamsters' local. The union struck because the company refused to yield to the excessive demands and uncompromising posture of the union. The union leadership kept telling the members that the company would buckle, as it had in the past. But the union was wrong because the company had already figured out that it couldn't pay what the employees demanded and still earn a profit. And the company had learned that it could benefit financially by selling its assets and closing down.

I remember one negotiation session when we discussed the company's threat to liquidate. The union officials laughed and said, "It's a bluff. They'll never do it." I can remember the snicker — it was almost an "I dare you" — on the faces of the union's bargaining committee. But the company made good on its threat and went out of business.

But while the strike was in progress, the company had filed unfair labor charges against the union, claiming that it was threatening employees and refusing to bargain in good faith. Despite our efforts to urge the NLRB to move as expeditiously as possible, the case simply dragged on at a snail's pace. Then, after the company went out of business, I received a call from the NLRB, telling me that it had scheduled a trial and wanted to prosecute the union. It was, needless to say, too little and too late. The trial never took place. The witnesses are now scattered and even a company victory — or indirectly a victory for its employees — would be a hollow one. There is nothing to bargain about with the union anymore.

Sometimes it seems that the NLRB behaves as though it doesn't know that it is there to assure fair and honest dealings on both sides. That appeared to be the situation in an NLRB case that involved a bakery company. The government investigated the concern and found that it had violated the law by discharging employees for their pro-union activity. When the investigation was completed and settlement discussions were held, I heard that the employer settled for more than the employees lost in back wages. That was satisfactory to the NLRB. I think the agency should have tried to work out a more equitable settlement. Instead, its attitude appeared to be that it was the employer's decision and if he was willing to pay more than he should, that was his business. It was simply a case of double standards. But who acted on behalf of the employer? Not the NLRB.

Beyond all that, there is still another reason why the manner in which the Federal government involves itself in labor relations is dangerous. I am drawing on my personal experiences both as a former field investigator and, later, as a trial attorney for the NLRB, and I am writing after having dealt with the agency's trial attorneys for nearly twenty years. The reason I cite all that experience is that I realize that what I am now going to say will be resented by some people in government.

In my opinion many of the younger attorneys who work for the Federal agencies feel that if a violation of the law can be found, the trial attorney — often those very attorneys — will become involved, have an opportunity to try the case and to prosecute the employer. They enthusiastically seek glory and justify their actions on the grounds that they are gaining valuable experience. I know; I was there. I heard it. And I saw it. The fact that it is at the expense of the employer is of no consequence.

But, in what appears to be the beginning of a turnaround for the NLRB, its more recent balancing of the scales in favor of management drew a surprising blast from Lane Kirkland, the AFL-CIO chief. He declared in 1984 that the union movement might be better off if the NLRB were to disappear, our present labor laws scrapped, and labor-management relations returned to "the law of the jungle." His assertion was in part a reaction to the fact that the Board has acted against labor's secondary boycotts and that, freed of the agency's restraint, unions would be able to pressure more companies into recognizing them.

As Steven Greenhouse reported in The New York Times of February 19, 1985, "Since Mr. Kirkland made that remark, lawyers for both sides of the labor-management struggle have squared off over his suggestion that unions would have far more success organizing workers if both labor and management were to use their raw economic might, rather than the NLRB, in trying to overpower each other."

Added Greenhouse, "The head of the American Federation of Labor and Congress of Industrial Organizations well knows that the labor movement had not been a rousing success at organizing workers in recent years. Whenever employees vote on the issue of whether to unionize their workplace, labor loses such elections more than half the time. What is more, union membership fell to just 18.8 percent of the nation's work force in 1984, down from 23 percent in 1980. And Mr. Kirkland fears things will get worse for unions as President Reagan appoints more conservatives to the NLRB...."

The New York Times quotes Samuel Estreicher, a labor law professor at New York University as saying, "The NLRB may be chilling the success rate of unions, but that still doesn't explain the overall problem. They have a real image problem." But Professor Estreicher said that he doubted that Kirkland's proposal would accomplish much and that scrapping the agency would increase conflict.

"We have to move away from conflict in this country," Professor Estreicher said. "Returning to the law of the jungle would be moving in the wrong direction. We have to work toward increased cooperation, to help make jobs more fulfilling and to give workers greater participation in management."

For a Little History

In colonial years and for decades afterward the goals of labor legislation were diametrically opposed to what they are today. Laws were aimed at disciplining workers and restricting their freedom. Early statutes kept wages to a minimum and precluded worker organizations which would have supported and fostered worker needs. But a lid on earnings could hardly be effective or permanent in a republic where the economy grew rapidly and where labor was needed. And labeling worker amalgamation as a conspiracy was antithetical to a new country where work on the soil and in the factory was commonplace and essential. The vestiges of the feudal system which carried over to the colonies had to give way and did, yielding laws that nurtured better working conditions and productivity.

Legislation for labor's benefit first took hold in the states which created a ragtag of ordinances. As the country matured and interstate commerce, which the Constitution empowers Congress to control, grew, the weight and scope of labor legislation increasingly moved to the Federal level. This trend progressed and reached its heights in the twentieth century through a number of seminal laws.

In 1933, the National Industrial Recovery Act (NIRA) created at least temporarily a national shorter work week, minimum wages, better minimum age standards, and health and safety standards. In 1935, the National Labor Relations Act, also known as the Wagner Act, set up for the first time Federal recognition that workers had a right to organize and bargain collectively with management. The 1933 NIRA was declared unconstitutional in 1935, but this action left a strong, lingering demand that the Federal government act to regulate wages and hours. In 1938, the Fair Labor Standards Act was passed by Congress, setting wage and hour standards for workers employed in interstate or foreign commerce or engaged in producing goods used in those activities. From that law, which was amended in 1956, a precedent was set for Federal minimum wages and for wages to be earned in overtime hours beyond the basic forty hour week.

In 1936, the Federal Public Contracts Act, also known as the Walsh-Healey Act, was passed. It applied to employers with government contracts higher than $10,000 in value. It required them to pay the prevailing Federal minimum wage, to pay overtime wages, and not to employ boys under sixteen or girls under eighteen. Retaining and reinforcing some of the major provisions of the discarded NIRA, the National Labor Relations Act put some teeth into labor's rights. It prevented employers from engaging in practices which hampered labor organizing, erected election machinery to settle disputes on employee representation, and established the National Labor Relations Board to police these rules.

But, in order to remove some of its teeth, the Act was changed in 1947 and renewed as the Labor Management Relations Act, also known as the Taft-Hartley Act. It continued the right of collective bargaining, retained a listing of unfair labor practices by employers, and added unfair labor practices committed by unions. The new law removed some of the sting of its predecessor by increasing the NLRB from three to five members and bestowed final authority on the general counsel, rather than the Board itself, for the investigation and prosecution of unfair labor charges.

Under Taft-Hartley, the Federal Mediation and Conciliation Service was set up to aid management and labor to reach a resolution of labor disputes. Mostly the Service intervenes only when there appears to be a major disruption of interstate commerce.

There were other Federal labor laws enacted, such as the 1932 Norris-LaGuardia Act defining the powers of the Federal courts to issue injunctions in labor disputes and the 1947 Labor Management Relations Act which established prenotification regulations on employers and unions which intended to change or void collective bargaining agreements. But the others were the major laws involving the government in labor relations and were paralleled by a number of state laws.

It is clear, however, even in a superficial review that American labor legislation is definitely slanted toward labor, despite the Taft-Hartley Act and labor's frequent contention that "it ain't necessarily so."

What about other countries?

Obviously, the developed countries of the world have taken a more enlightened position to protect worker's rights than have the underdeveloped countries. In fact, the amount of enforcement varies directly among both the developed and the underdeveloped countries and is based not only on their economic achievement but also on the strength of their labor movements and on the country's tradition of law enforcement. In many cases, Japan being an exception, both legislation and enforcement have followed the example of the United States, so that the right of workers as a group to communicate their views on employment conditions has become the general rule. But in underdeveloped countries, the thrust of enforcement has been blunted toward smaller businesses and sharpened toward the large ones. In most countries, the basic workweek has been limited to between forty and forty-eight hours, with at least one day of rest. A minimum employment age has been generally established except in family businesses. And worker health standards have been established to varying degrees.

In Communist countries, wages have been put under control, integrated with government goals for economic growth, and some incentives have been provided. Wage rates have been set low to make it necessary for both husband and wife to work in order to keep as many people as possible in the labor force. In consumer goods industries, wages are kept even lower with a higher wage level in producer industries so as to steer workers toward the latter rather than the former since industrial goods represent the countries' prime developmental effort.

Conversely, most non-Communist countries have adopted minimum wage laws. Such legislation also provides for wage boards which consist of labor, management, and the public or the government. The boards periodically set wage levels for different occupations. In some developed countries in which there is significant unionism, the minimum wage rates set by collective bargaining have taken the place of legislated wages.

Although wartime governmental strictures on prices, rationing, and subsidies were later abandoned, vestiges of some of these controls still remain in some countries. Nationwide collective agreements fix wage levels pegged to the cost of living in Italy, Belgium, and Denmark. In France the government changes the minimum wage when prices rise 5 percent. Pay rate changes in

Australia are tied by arbitration to retail price changes. In such Eastern countries as India, Pakistan, and Sri Lanka, cost-of-living allowances are kept as part of the wage structure and change when consumer prices rise or fall.

Legislation providing unemployment insurance to protect workers against loss of income due to loss of employment has been enacted by such countries as Japan, the Union of South Africa, the non-Communist European countries, Canada, and Yugoslavia. Other nations in Latin America and Asia have taken further steps to curb unemployment, with laws prohibiting or complicating discharge of unneeded workers. Where dismissals are allowed, the employer must pay from two to four weeks wages for each year of service. And in many of these countries striking workers continue to be paid by the employer. This practice costs the employer less than severance to discharge the worker. Custom in those countries also calls for the employer to shoulder that responsibility.

Thus, it isn't hard to discern that the American system of government protection for labor and involvement in management-labor relations isn't as enlightened as might be thought.

But it is our contention that this is not such a bad thing at all. Why? Because the more government involvement there is, the more socialistic and pro-labor the country's policy becomes. If there would be governmental machinery to control not just the unfair practices of employers, but the excessive demands of unions and their aggravated protests and strikes, government involvement might be a good thing.

The most vivid contrast to our own policies in labor relations exists in Japan.

"Tetuo Ohsone, the top labor union official at the Toyo Kogyo Company, gives a visitor a small gift, a tie clip," wrote John Holusha, automotive industry writer for The New York Times in the May 30, 1983, issue. Reporting during a visit to Hiroshima, he went on, "Prominently displayed on it is the word, 'Mazda,' the trade name for Toyo Kogyo cars, and a symbol depicting the company's unique rotary engine. The union's initials are barely discernable.

"Mr. Ohsone's gesture indicates the close links that unions in Japan have with automobile companies. In Detroit, confrontation had marked labor-management relationships ever since members of the United Automobile Workers Union sang 'solidarity forever, the union makes us strong' as they fought to organize and struck for better wages. In Japan, assembly line workers have long been encouraged to feel they are as much a part of the company as the president.

"As a result," Holusha continued, "during the past two decades of rapid growth, the Japanese auto industry has been untroubled by the long strikes that were regular events in Detroit in the 1970s. And Japanese auto workers have become known the world over for their attention to quality, low absentee rates and willingness to shift from one job to another as needed. The auto companies have responded with steadily rising wages and fringe benefits, including subsidized housing and a no-layoff policy...."

No contrast, it seems, could be more striking than the situations in Japan and in the U.S. But it is also evident that the difference stems naturally from the different historical backgrounds of both countries. But there's an irony in it, too. The Japanese government and employers do not mind taking a paternal attitude toward workers, more or less guaranteeing them lifetime employment, and the workers are generally happy to accept that role. In the U.S. there has always been an intrinsic sense of support for "the little guy." We always seem to be a country that favors the underdog while the employer has always been viewed as "the big guy." The result has been a tug-of-war that has continued for decades.

It's likely, though, that this lingering management-labor strife could have been circumvented by more constructive employer policies and employee interaction. If employers had not made the mistake of abusing and ignoring their workers so much in the earlier decades of the twentieth century, the relationships might have been much better. The long-entrenched perception of sweatshops has so tainted our view of American management that the general public and, more specifically, the working public will never forget the horrible image. The Federal government, it seems, has been preoccupied with ensuring that the sweatshops era will never recur. That's not a bad thing at all. Employers, humane considerations aside, certainly can't operate sweatshops today if they want high productivity. We are way beyond those days and should be. But there is another dimension to it.

While it is not an intrinsically bad concept for a particular employer to have an edge, it is also not bad to somewhat disadvantage the large employer economically when dealing with the Federal bureaucracy. But the idea that an employer can pay back wages more easily than the employee can suffer these losses does not really wash in the world of the 1980s. It's not at all certain that an idea like that ever had a real place in America. Those who advocate that "the little guy," the employee, should always be given the advantage in labor relations have had their day in the sun. That attitude prevailed for a long time and the country did prosper from the 1940s through the early 1970s. It worked then, but can it work now?

The answer is as obvious as the unhappy economic indicators of the late 1970s and the early 1980s. It does *not* work. The erroneous "favor the little guy" approach combined with the intensifying adversarial relationship between management and labor caused the American economy to plummet in the early 1980s to its worst state since the 1930s. Where is "the little guy" — in fact where has he gone — when the companies that once provided jobs became part of the dustbin of business history?

Other countries. When we look at other industrialized countries, such as Great Britain, Canada, France, and Italy, where government involvement in labor relations has been deep and socialistic in nature, it is obvious that the effect has not been positive or productive. In Britain and Canada the government bureaucracy certainly has been an extension of the arm of unions and employees. In England the Thatcher government has sought to reverse this relationship, but it has been very difficult to reverse the errors of the past. The result has been one of the worst economic periods in Britain's history. In Canada the labor laws are structured to limit employer power and to give advantages to labor.

In the U.S. a union becomes an authorized bargaining agency for a company's employees by winning an NLRB-conducted election. The union can also be the beneficiary of a bargaining order issued by the Board against the employer after a Board-conducted hearing. And the union can also become the bargaining agent if an employer voluntarily recognizes the union after ascertaining that the majority of employees signed valid authorization cards.

But in Canada, when employees sign union cards, if a specified majority of cards is obtained by the union, it can take them

to the provincial labor board and obtain certification as the bargaining agent on the basis of membership evidence rather than by a secret ballot election. The employer then has the burden to show that
the union does not truly represent the employees. The employer
might, for example, assert that the authorization cards were forged,
a difficult thing to show, and if he can't establish that, the union
automatically becomes the legally certified bargaining agent for the
employees. The fallacy of authorization card majorities, in Canada
as well as in the U.S., involves the pressures that underlie the signing of union cards. Fear, peer pressure, superior proselytizing by
the union rather than by management, work in favor of the "yes"
answer, so that the mere signing of a card doesn't necessarily indicate the employee's true intent. That aside, it has been generally
recognized that in Canada, Great Britain—and in our our own
country—the very favorable pro-union labor laws or at least pro-
employee labor laws have materially contributed to inflation.

A totally different policy prevails in Japan. A constructive
interaction is evident among the Japanese, their government, their
industry, and their labor unions. All elements of that country's
society clearly recognize that the capitalistic structure is paramount
and that without it considerably fewer jobs would exist. The government's support of big business is one of the major reasons
Japanese business can compete so effectively in the international
marketplace. This can only work because Japanese workers respect
their coworkers, their superiors, and their plant perhaps more than
in any other country. Management in its turn has a deep, pro-
prietary attitude toward the workers, assuming responsibility for
their well-being, employment, health, and safety. The mutual
solicitude makes for strong morale on both sides, creating ties that
last for generations through children and even grandchildren.

As a result, employees are willing to work hard and produce
and employers do not regard them as a necessary evil but as true
members of the business or production family. Is the class structure
of our American environment so rigid that we will never achieve
that degree of rapport? Implicitly, the very ego which perhaps has
given us our classic American drive would get in the way of that
sort of closely knit partnership between management and labor.
Perhaps we do not want or need that partnership. But, in order to
avoid becoming a second-class power, we must have a new climate

of partnership and mutual consideration, not Japanese-style but American-style. We need a partnership that reaches across the bargaining table for the mutual benefit of management and labor.

The fact is, socialism, undue government influence in management-labor activities, and pro-labor laws simply haven't worked. Our own pro-labor legislation has not been able to avoid periods of sky-high inflation and the worst unemployment since the 1930s. Japan is beginning to feel it, too, particularly as the younger segment begins to tear the constricting fabric of traditional government-business-labor unity. Extremes, it seems, never really work, unless one wants to ignore the hunger for freedom that lives, however submerged in human beings.

It isn't even necessary to dwell on the Soviet Union and its satellites, where the Communist ideology's survival is the paramount necessity and individual freedom (not to mention the needs of business or workers) is a considerably lesser priority.

So what does an international score card reveal? The amity of business and workers, with the exception of Japan and perhaps West Germany to a much lesser extent, is hardly notable anywhere in the world. Government involvement whether slanted toward business, as in Japan (where unionism and anti-business agitation are on the rise) or toward labor, as in the U.S., France, and Italy, becomes increasingly questionable in terms of sustaining production or curbing inflation. In the U.S. our government involvement is more primitive than enlightened, more one-sided in favor of labor than even-handed. What we sorely need is both less government involvement and more of a partnership between management and labor to establish a common front against mutual problems, principally the worsening climate between the two forces.

Earlier I mentioned that government involvement might yet be worthwhile if we had a facility or vehicle within the government machinery to curb excessive demands made by unions, or, for that matter, by business. Some suggestions along those lines:

1.   A Presidential commission empowered to recommend new laws to provide some balance and wisdom to ever-churning relationships of management and labor might well provide some wholesome benefits. It's been several decades since the enactment of the amendments to the Taft-Hartley Act. A new reality exists and a new attitude is needed.

Clearly, traditional attitudes among Americans, whether in government, management, or labor, will not be lightly changed, certainly not in the near term. And that is worrisome. As a society, we have been given an economic reprieve. We are bailing ourselves out of an economic crisis, but we are still in trouble. Unless our attitudes change quickly and we recognize the problems of the recent past, our economy is going to run out of chances for successful recovery in the future.

2.   If a Presidential commission is formed, perhaps one of the things that could emerge from it would be a law that provides access to more government decisions. The Freedom of Information Act seems to work effectively for the media when it presses for disclosure. But why can't the laws be structured to compel regulatory agencies to disclose how and why they arrive at their decisions. Is it possible that the threat of forced disclosure will pressure agency officials at all decision-making levels to act more objectively?

3.   Many of the current labor laws, including the much touted Labor Anti-Racketeering Act, bear an adversarial thrust in and of themselves. They are designed to pit one part of our society against another. While in some respects this may provide the effect of a check and balance, perhaps we should think instead of enacting more positive laws that do not contain this built-in adversarial process.

4.   Another less political agency might be empowered to investigate or review on an appeal basis decisions of some of the other agencies and to render a decision in no more than thirty days. That could be an alternative to expanding the disclosure laws under the Freedom of Information Act. Such an impartial reviewing body in the labor-management field could exert the power to enjoin agency action, peremptory business demands, strikes, and thereby act as a defusing arm for brewing labor-management conflicts. Its charter would make it explicit that the agency would have the defusing authority and that its chairman would be directly responsible to the President. Or there could be a bipartisan unit such as the Watergate Investigating Commission. These could, of course, be tied to the expanding Presidential power permitted under the emergency injunctive provisions of the Taft-Hartley Act.

Big Brother? Not really. If the law gives the agency or commission the right to act against either business or labor, its policing would be equitable. Big Referee is more like it.

CHAPTER V

HOW TO IGNORE THE LESSONS OF HISTORY

A scorpion wanted to cross a river on the back of a frog. When the scorpion asked the frog to take him across the river, the frog replied, "I can't do that because you will sting me and I will die." The scorpion said, "Of course, I won't sting you because if I sting you in the middle of the river and you die, I will die, too." The frog said, "That seems logical. I will take you across." But halfway across the river, the scorpion bit the frog. As the frog was dying, he said to the scorpion, "I'm dying. Why did you bite me? We are both going to drown." The scorpion replied: "I know. But that is my character. I don't know any different."

I n mid-1983 the long forgotten became the all too familiar. Too often the glowing promises made under pressure are, sadly enough, not delivered. We have all seen it happen, time and again.

After three days of discussion at Hot Springs, Virginia, the corporate members of the Business Council, the one hundred or so heads of America's biggest corporations, solemnly disclosed that they would rehire few of the workers whom they had laid off during the recession. This would be the case, they insisted, no matter how strongly the economy picked up.

James H. Evans, chairman of the Union Pacific Corporation, the huge transportation company, said that the company had laid off 6,000 of its 44,000 employees and probably wouldn't bring them back. Speaking to The New York *Times*, he added: "We're running 40 percent more freight tonnage than we did 20 years ago, with half as many employees. If we had the same number of employees we had then, we would have priced ourselves out of the market. How have we done it? Automation."

Edward G. Jefferson, chairman of E.I. Du Pont de Nemours & Company, told the newspaper that Du Pont's capacity to produce synthetic fibers had doubled the 1973 level, but "the manpower to operate is up only 4 to 5 percent because of mechanization of robotics."

Du Pont had laid off 7 percent of its worldwide work force of 174,000 during the recession, Jefferson said. But in a booming economy, he added, "just a few" would be rehired.

More of the same sad tale was predicted for the automotive industry. As the nation started its eighth postwar recovery, *Business Week* told its readers, the outlook for employment in the auto industry was bleak. "The combination of modest demand, import competition and stepped-up automation means that we are going to have fewer people than we had before," Alfred S. Warren, Jr., vice president for industrial relations at General Motors Corporation, told the magazine. This is likely to have a depressing effect for years, according to *Business Week*, not only on the United Auto Workers but also on other industries and communities whose economic health is tied to autos.

So, the first development which brought the present and future face-to-face with the past was the fact that there existed no established equation between laid-off workers and improved economic times. It is true that better economic conditions generally reduce the jobless rate. However, the realities of the last quarter of the twentieth century are that ever-growing international competition, increased automation and robotics, and the decline of union membership have tended to offset job reinvigoration. After the 1974-1975 recession, the U.S. jobless rate rose to 8.5 percent. It remained in the 9 to 11 percent range for several years afterward.

Also, in 1983, a task force of sixteen heads of major universities and corporations urged President Reagan to place the imprimatur and weight of the White House behind a national program to restore the country's ability to compete with other industrial nations. Convened by the President, the task force of the

Business-Higher Education Forum declared that such a restoration must become the country's "central objective" for the rest of the decade. The task force found that:

Other nations have recognized the new economic imperative, and have integrated their domestic and foreign policies into aggressive, coordinated national strategies to meet the challenge of international competition. The United States on the other hand has not . . . As a nation, we must develop a consensus that industrial competitiveness is crucial to our social and economic well-being. Strengthening America's ability to compete will require exceptional resources, patience, sacrifice and vision. It will require avoiding the twin pitfalls of protectionism and increased government intervention into private sector activities.

Among the recommendations of the task force were modifications of antitrust laws so that companies could cooperate in sponsoring basic research, further reductions in the capital gains tax on long-term investments, federal loans for graduate engineering students who agree to become teachers, and development of a "displaced worker program modeled after the GI Bill."

The task force added: "Despite the fact that the United States has the world's largest capital base, the world's most advanced technology and a highly educated and skilled work force, there is a disturbing evidence that the nation is failing to utilize these strengths fully."

The report, entitled "America's Competitive Challenge: The Need for a National Response," was signed by the sixteen who formed the task force. The co-chairmen were Robert Anderson, chairman of the Rockwell International Corporation, and David S. Saxon, president of the University of California. One of the study's most compelling points was that restoring the ability of American industry to compete in international markets "would require the same national consensus that allowed the United States to land men on the moon."

The task force, seeking immediate action—which it did not get—suggested several ways of dealing with "the nature and severity of the competitive challenge." The task force suggested that

President Reagan make a major public address describing, challenging, and recommending ways of achieving international competitiveness; he should appoint a Presidential Advisor on Economic Competitiveness similar to those in the fields of national security and science; he should staff a previously announced National Commission on Industrial Competitiveness to coordinate national efforts of that kind; and he should establish an Information Center on International Competitiveness in the Commerce Department to facilitate the flow of information relating to economic growth.

Among many other proposals, the task force recommended tax incentives for corporations to retrain workers displaced by technological change.

Obviously, there was ample reason for the task force's study. Moreover, the considerable deliberation and seriousness of the group's recommendations certainly warranted action by the White House and the nation.

But studies conducted by White House task forces or Presidential commissions all too often have very little effect. Usually, the ideas submitted by such groups receive momentary acclaim and then are tossed into the bottom drawer of the President's desk or more probably that of one of his many assistants. Occasionally, the findings, such as those of the President's Productivity Commission, surface at business conventions for a brief airing and then are relegated to the dustbin of history. Some are undoubtedly valuable. But one cannot escape the feeling that putting together such blue-chip groups and announcing their conclusions are directed more towards calling the matter to the attention of the appropriate industries or institutions than towards prompting action from the White House.

Sometimes Presidential task forces even cancel out one another. Such was the case involving the group assembled by President Lyndon Johnson in the late sixties and headed by Dean Phil C. Neal of the University of Chicago to study whether the antitrust laws were outmoded by the raging trend of conglomerates. Rather than urging an attack on conglomerates, the Neal group urged an attack on oligopolies by introducing new legislation designed to break up big companies. But by the time that the Neal task force could release its findings, a task force convened by President Richard Nixon and headed by Professor George J. Stigler of the

University of Chicago delivered its own recommendations. The Stigler Commission took issue with the Neal panel's push against oligopolies, instead urging a probe of such companies—and more specifically, one that would investigate the detrimental effects of pricing on competition.

The split made life difficult for the regulatory agencies and confused the public. There's no doubt that such high level studies serve a purpose by calling attention to major national problems, but almost always they result in little overt action. Something may yet emerge from the Anderson-Saxon group's recommendations for reviving the U.S. competitive challenge. But for those in both management and labor looking for leadership or direction to attack the national problem of fading American leadership in the world marketplace, the much publicized series of proposals bore the hollow echo of many earlier unproductive efforts of a similar variety.

Another development that emerged in May, 1983, was the large membership losses of many American labor unions.

As reported by The New York *Times* national labor reporter William Serrin, most experts predicted that many of the losses would be permanent because the unions hit by major membership declines were connected with industries that will not have the huge employment that they enjoyed in the past. Data from the Bureau of National Affairs reveal that union membership is in the midst of a steady downward spiral. In 1980, 20.1 million union workers comprised 23 percent of the nation's labor force. In 1983, the figure was 17.7 million, or 20.1 percent of the work force. Unions hit bottom in 1984, as figures demonstrate there were 17.3 million union workers, which equates to a mere 18.8 percent of the nation's labor force.

Specifics: Membership at the United Automobile Workers by the mid-1980s was down to 1.1 million, 27 percent below the 1.5 million in the 1970s. The United Steelworkers of America reported that its membership had dropped 42 percent to 750,000, from more than 1.3 million in the late 1970s. The United Rubber Workers of America said that its rolls had declined 31 percent to 125,000, against a 1978 total of 180,000.

International Brotherhood of Teamsters membership was down 22 percent to 1.8 million, compared with 2.3 million in the late 1970s. The International Ladies Garment Workers Union listed

283,000 members, 17 percent lower than the 341,000 it had in 1979. The International Association of Machinists said that its rolls fell 39 percent to under 600,000, from a 1969 high of 986,000. But the United Mine Workers of America said its membership of 230,000 was somewhat up in recent years. Yet, by comparison with its 1942 total of 595,000, the 1980 membership was pitifully low. Finally, the American Federation of Labor and Congress of Industrial Organizations said that its membership, consisting of ninety-nine affiliated unions, had dropped to 13.7 million, from a projected 14.9 million in early 1982, and that more declines were expected.

The erosion of union support is continuing and is expected to last a long time. Jerome M. Rosow, president of Work in America Institute, Inc., a private research organization in Scarsdale, New York, observed that declining union membership demonstrates that the union movement "is pretty much locked into heavy, old industry" and has "not moved in the direction of high-tech and other new industries." In addition, he told Serrin, companies have been moving to the South and Southwest, not union strongholds, and "today many companies pay relatively high wages and benefits to thwart unions. Many American workers are better educated than before and do not identify with unions. The only union growth has come among government workers."

All of these statistics reveal the past revisited. At least four times in the past decades union membership had declined because of reverses in economic trends. Inflation and overexpansion of American industry had worked their destabilizing effects on organized labor. In 1926, union membership fell to 3,502,000, from a high of 5,048,000 in 1920. In the trough of the Depression, 1933, the rolls had dwindled to only 2,857,000 members, from a then high of 3,632,000 in 1930. The membership level was the lowest since 1916. In the late 1940s and 1950s, as industrial expansion thundered along to fill the pipelines emptied by the impact of World War II, there was a three-year plateau in which union membership totaled only 15,000,000, dropping 414,000 from the 1947 level. In 1961, the total fell to 17,328,000, from a then high of 18,477,000 in 1956.

In other words, union membership fluctuated with the capriciousness of supply and demand, economic cycles, and competition from imports. Neither labor's assurances nor management's blue-sky promises guaranteed any stability in the curve of labor's enrollment. It is easy to forget this, to overlook it amid the propaganda and hyperbole offered by each side.

Those three developments reached the public's perception in the late spring of 1983 as the White House sent out glowing pronouncements of not only the end of the recession but of a gathering economic boom. With the nation eagerly awaiting such news, it's unlikely that the public — or management and labor — realized that history has a way of repeating itself and that those whose will to survive and, indeed, improve their lot should be listening to the lessons that slide beneath the layers of history.

Noodling through History

Perhaps no one flouted history's lessons more than management and labor as they kept repeating their mistakes during the last few decades.

Management certainly has made its share of errors. As I have discussed in previous chapters, business so enjoyed making its profits in the marketplace that it allowed several priorities to slide. Business has been both soft and weak in maintaining a practical economic stance as far as labor relations and labor costs are concerned. While inflation was on the rise and productivity on the decline, management didn't seem much concerned as long as the bottom line was improving. The result of the "let's not rock the boat" attitude and behavior was economic and industrial stagnation.

Labor, too, made its share of errors. During the 1950s and 1960s when unions successfully obtained larger and larger economic gains, a bandwagon rolled through American society. The feeling in the workplace grew that the one sure way of getting wage increases was to have the union behind you. Organized labor seemed to have a winning formula and took full advantage of it. There was a certain euphoria about it, too. Within the system, business, labor, and workers were all plugging away in the same vein, despite some incipient antagonism and some strikes, happy in the loose check-and-balance arrangement, because in the end everyone was getting a piece of the action.

Inside the labor movement, relatively new trends were emerging — ones that hadn't surfaced for some decades, after earlier internecine battling among rival unions. Although members of the giant AFL-CIO were organized within craft and industry units, the Teamsters, previously almost exclusively a trucking union, began to organize an industrial-manufacturing complex, crossing over into other types of employment. It was simply unheard of for the Teamsters to organize office-clericals, but because the Teamsters needed members, it began staking out new claims.

Additionally, unions were moving steadily towards organizing employees in growing white collar and service industries, where the focus of our economy was shifting. Also, unions began initiating mergers in order to strengthen their appeal.

Talk about an adversarial relationship! Quite suddenly a new dimension had entered management-labor relations. Not only were employers battling with a particular union within an industry, but unions were now fighting with one another to gain or keep their share of employee representation. Not only were the Teamsters, for example, able to organize any available employees, but the Steelworkers and other unions also began making their own forays into the white-collar market. Shrinking membership left unions with no alternative but to organize unorganized workers in every sector of society. They were also willing to raid other unions where workers had been organized under a particular union umbrella for many years.

This new ingredient was hardly destined to help matters. It served, and still serves, to add to the heat of the "Us against Them" hard-line approach that had already hurt so much. But interunion rivalry had even greater ramifications.

America is undergoing a shift from manufacturing to non-manufacturing service industries as the major component in its economy. Many service industries now have gross revenues that are larger than some of the traditional manufacturing industries. The most promising new area is, of course, the high-technology industries, the new frontier that may well form the foundation for future economic growth in the U.S. High-tech industries may give America its second chance to truly regain world economic stature and even leadership. If that happens, it is reasonable to assume that major problems such as high unemployment can be lessened. But, given the raiding and new organizing of labor unions entering the high-tech and white-collar fields, which are characterized by the same old promises to potential new members, the same sort of problems could well be transferred from earlier decades into the new areas of endeavor on which America's future may be based. It can only perpetuate the "We/They" syndrome.

Labor, however, may not feel that it has a choice. If it is to survive, it needs new members. Fresh new organizing not only provides numbers but also gives the tired, eroded union a new breath and a new morale. But, if high-tech is to be the new campaign terrain for organized labor, will its leaders be wise or, for that matter, sensible enough to refrain from pushing the same excessive demands in spite of economic realities? Can the public ask that? The answer is that it should and it must.

Moreover, will corporate America be able to face up to that new challenge? At this juncture, it's hard to say. But what is immediately worrisome is that it appears likely that American businessmen won't rise to the challenge quickly enough. If they were given enough time, they would probably face up to it successfully. But it's like a time bomb, and you can hear it ticking.

Lane Kirkland, the head of the AFL-CIO, has begun to target certain industries and certain areas of the country to make up for membership that the union lost. He claims that the AFL-CIO has invested $1 million to organize in the city of Houston alone. Purportedly, the union has also set aside the same amount to tackle other cities such as Atlanta.

Obviously, the new organizing will take the pattern of the union's traditional drive — it will seek the biggest wage gains it can get. That is the only way organized labor feels it can sell itself to the unorganized worker.

But — if we are to learn the lessons of history — we must ask ourselves whether we have the option of making wage gains in industries such as high technology the major thrust in building a better economic society. To the contrary, the emphasis must be on productivity, especially if the aim is to build a stronger, more competitive economy that will wield more clout in the international marketplace. Will labor unions hear the message and listen? Their survival may be at stake. Inevitably, the burden falls on management, whether unions listen or not.

But whether management will accept that burden is a matter of concern. As I travel around the U.S. and talk to many in corporate

America, I try to emphasize the new direction of labor unions as they zero in on the new, unorganized areas. For example, not only has the Communications Workers of America targeted major companies in the communications field, but with the current trend toward deregulation, the union is also expanding its view to include a broader marketplace. The United Food and Commercial Workers is planning to organize companies in a number of new industries. But what I hear in response to all this is downright frightening. After a talk I gave to executives in the New England health-care industry, these executives told me in so many words: "Mr. Cabot, we're not particularly concerned." They explained that the economy has been so bad that unions won't be successful in their organizing. I also hear that corporate America is so busy with its own economic adjustments that it can't worry about some of the "potential problems" that may occur even if they are important.

When I bring up issues such as white-collar organizing or unions lining up the new professional employees, the impression I get is employers feel that "it can't happen to me." This implies that if it does happen, which, they feel, is not a certainty, "it will happen to the guy across the street." And if it does happen to him, "well, then I'm going to have enough time to prepare myself for the struggle." This attitude, unfortunately, runs counter to the lessons that management should have learned from the past.

At the root of this very unrealistic attitude is another lesson from history that is being overlooked, the fact that employees intrinsically feel they are being exploited. It takes time and actions for management to achieve credibility with their workers. Even with actions and an open, cooperative atmosphere, it takes time. But, sadly, we find that too many companies in American industry turn a deaf ear to the needs and wishes of their white-collar and professional employees. Some employees are treated decently; many others are not paid enough or given the benefits that they should receive. Had it been otherwise, it would not have been so easy for the aggressive unions to have organized so well in the white-collar field.

A case in point. A company that we represent, a Fortune 500 producer with plants around the U.S., had a dual problem. It had been working overtime to keep its blue-collar force in one plant from accepting the blandishments of a major international union.

The situation was complicated by the fact that some of its union-ized plants were on strike. In addition, the company wanted to take back some of the benefits that the nonunionized blue-collar workers enjoyed. That decision, difficult at best in that context, was the first problem.

The second problem was that the company also wanted to cut the wages and benefits of the white-collar workers in the non-unionized plant by 10 percent. Wavering on the takebacks from the unorganized blue-collar employees, the company initially decided that the blue-collar workers at the unorganized plant would not give up anything. And this idea stuck. Despite the obvious unfair-ness of taking back wages and benefits from the white-collar workers, who were not under union attack, but not from the blue-collar workers who were being wooed by the union, the company still decided to discriminate between the two groups. It tried to finesse the issue by sweet-talking the white-collar employees, but they were not taken in.

Those workers are now, of course, sitting ducks for a union to organize them. But perhaps more importantly, the white-collar workers are now sharply alienated from management. In other words, the "We/They" approach has taken over with respect to those employees. It's a serious question whether management can ever restore its credibility with the workers, if it was ever there in the first place.

This is a clear case of management deluding itself. Manage-ment completely miscalculates the effect of its policies on the blue-collar group. Seeing how management can mistreat another group of workers, the blue-collar people can only distrust management, even though they were not hurt in the process. One of the top managers in the plant flatly asserted that preference should be given to blue-collar workers because they were directly involved in producing the profits that made the plant viable, while the white-collar people were in effect only support troops. Underlying this comment is a point he failed to mention. His bonus is based upon the productivity of the blue-collar group but not directly on the white-collar people.

It is evident that if the company's discriminatory attitude per-sists, all the workers at the plant will lose, not just one group.

Rational common sense has vanished. The union position is

hardening around the conviction that unless it does what it has to, it will not survive. Management is convinced that if the unions continue their adversarial approach to business, no one will survive. Without question, it's time for a return to fundamentals, to summon up the clear-eyed pragmatism of Samuel Gompers, who said that the worst crime a company can commit against its workers is not to make a profit. Axiomatically, when companies make profits, workers have jobs, and even unions prosper while our economy thrives. But as business's profits erode, the effects are reversed.

Let me step back a bit to bring the labor-management relationship up to date before attempting some recommendations.

From the Middle Ages to the first third of the twentieth century, workers everywhere wanted to cut the number of hours they worked and eventually succeeded in reducing them by 50 percent. In the U.S., as business grew and abuses mounted, workers organized with the approval of government. Two societies flourished, the business and the labor establishments, both working well within the capitalistic system. But as the emphasis shifted from hours to wages, fringes, and other benefits, the bonus became greater. In the second half of the 1970s, wage increases outpaced U.S. productivity by 7 percent. By permitting such wage gains, U.S business put itself into an untenable position. Business could not fight inflation and imports. Labor all but asked for a tougher stance to be taken by management when it made excessive demands. As long as collective bargaining could reap a portion of industry's profits, unions favored the capitalistic system. But when the system let them down in terms of high unemployment and takebacks, the promises of unionism went unfulfilled and unions became confused and more militant.

After the jobless rate had jumped to a forty-year high, it became painfully obvious that traditional employer-employee interaction was neither helping industrial output or sustaining employment. Even today national production lags as business grapples with a greater influx of foreign goods and investment and extensive Federal regulation. Capital outlays struggle to ignore uncertain prospects. And unions, losing membership, are abandoning traditional craft identifications, adding another element of struggle to an overall polarized system of management-labor relations.

How to Recoup on History's Lessons

In the 1980s and certainly beyond, workers, I believe, are becoming too sophisticated to truly believe in union rhetoric just as they have already learned to mistrust business' glowing promises.

The new workers, both organized and unorganized, will clearly remember that they were completely on their own in terms of overpromises by both sides. The union hierarchy said that we could get more and more from corporate America and the threats of plant closure were just empty. This rhetoric was patently nothing more than a significant act of union irresponsibility. Management was no less culpable, using givebacks as a wedge to cut employment while it prepared to install more and more automation and robotics. Obviously, unions must change their ways if they are to survive. But, out of frustration and desperation, they are reverting to the past, employing old techniques such as false promises to create unrealistic employee expectations. This will in the short term only encourage the adversarial relationship. Yet we must rid ourselves of that relationship if our economy is to gain a second breath and become a world force once more.

It can be done. If history proves anything, it is that a little initiative, a little courage, and a breadth of vision go a long way. The conduct of a union representative connected with a consumer product manufacturer in the Northeast whom we represented offers a good example of the vision that is needed today. The moral of the story should offer food for thought not only for unions but for management as well.

The company's management was in the process of automating its office procedures and switching to a computerized system. The Steelworkers' union, learning that the company's white-collar workers were concerned about the security of their jobs, began an organizing effort. Pressed to indicate how the automation would affect jobs, management wasn't candid or honest, mostly replying with untruths or not responding at all. Eventually, when the pressure mounted, management simply lied, telling the white-collar people that there would be no layoffs. Ultimately, as often happens when computers are installed, a series of layoffs began.

The workers, both those who were laid off and those who weren't, were understandably upset and the Steelworkers' union intensified its organizing campaign. But, in addition to the company's decline in credibility, there was another complication. The white-collar group happened to be very well paid in both wages and benefits. At a number of union meetings the union organizer was asked if the union would be able to get the workers improvements in wages and benefits.

He told them that the union would try, but he also reminded the white-collar employees that they were already being paid well above both area and industry standards. He said that he couldn't make any false promises, certainly promises that he was not sure the union could fulfill. But he went on to tell them about some of the company's abuses and mistakes, particularly its improper and even false communications. He did promise that if the Steelworkers' union was elected their bargaining agent, it would make sure that they were treated fairly. There would not be any credibility gap, he assured them. They would always have full access to all available information, and in general, he would do all in his power to see that they were treated fairly.

The employees, sobered by the entire situation, voted in favor of the union and shortly thereafter the NLRB certified the Steelworkers' union as the official bargaining representative of the workers.

Before that happened, at another union meeting, the employees asked the union rep whether the company could be prevented from asking for any further layoffs. He replied that the union couldn't guarantee how effectively it could do that. He added that the union would work with management to determine that all layoffs were fair and that all employees would be treated properly. There would be no unnecessary layoffs if the union could prevent it, he said. Implicit in what he was saying, of course, was that it wasn't necessarily in the best interest of all the employees, the company, or the union if the company's hands were tied in trying to operate efficiently. That meant that the workers and the union had to accept the fact that layoffs might be part of such a program.

Such candid statements took courage and an enlightened attitude. It also introduced a measure of sanity to the "We/They" approach. Carried further, such an attitude can be beneficial even in unpleasant situations where layoffs must be made. Working constructively with management, the union can discuss and make some input in such matters as the appropriate number of people to be laid off and the order in which this is to happen.

I believe that management would not only be receptive to this cooperative attitude in the 1980s, but it might even go a step further. This could well mean discussions with the union and its members about how people who are laid off can be retrained. Such a relationship can be of immense benefit. It is possible that programs of this type, widespread throughout American industry, might prove to be a real strength for the future for the U.S.

The case just related bears some lessons for management too. The simple but very clear revelation in it is that business is not going to be able to sweet-talk, soft-soap, or otherwise manipulate its employees to the degree that it has in the past. If today's employee is too sophisticated to absorb the union's old rhetoric, he is certainly going to be skeptical about the same product dispensed by the employer. The employees of the consumer products manufacturer were not really opposed to management making certain changes which were in the best interest of the company. But they absolutely rejected management when it lied to them or treated them as children. Lying to employees or trying to manipulate them will have a negative impact on labor relations.

Business can take an enlightened position. In New Jersey, where layoffs came in the wake of declining automobile sales in 1983, the problem has been tackled quite effectively. Car dealers in the state are now working with the major labor union which represents mechanics to develop a joint employer-union apprenticeship program. The goal is to train apprentices. But it is also being used to retrain employees who were laid off and give them a chance to be reemployed in a more skillful capacity. In the process, obviously, there is also the opportunity to impart new attitudes since the apprentices and retrained workers are being given a chance to develop and redevelop. It should never be too late to recall Samuel Gompers' principle, should it?

Problems also create opportunities. Perhaps as we look at the effect of robotics in terms of the displacement of employees, we can see the opportunity to emphasize training and retraining. Federal aid could be a positive force to fund apprenticeship training and the retraining of displaced workers. Such programs could be put under a joint employer-union umbrella.

Is it possible that a portion of the expected overall wage settlements in the next few years, which fall in the 6 to 7 percent range, might be set aside for use in apprenticeship and retraining programs? It could work, because with the employer, the union, and the workers all paying for it, the effort would enjoy a common goal.

There is one supremely significant lesson of history that we have forgotten in the entire area of American industry and labor. It is that we have lost our pride in workmanship, a characteristic that thrived in the United States from the time of our industrial revolution in the mid-nineteenth century. It carried over into the twentieth century and gave America its predominant competitive trade position throughout the world. It was dramatized during two World Wars and built a sense among us that what America made was the best anywhere. It was a conviction that we could do almost anything — and do it best. But sometime after World War II we lost much of the sense of pride in what we did and made and, in turn, the country lost or forgot an important ingredient in our history.

Today our industrial society seems to be engaged in a constant process of buck-passing. Labor blames management and management blames labor. The adversarial relationship thrives. But it is obvious that both sides are at fault. We are many times paralyzed by the feeling that the problems are large and seemingly insurmountable. The inevitable result is that everyone is afraid to make a decision. Even the fact that we have been so successful in the past compels many of us to do nothing so that we will not rock the boat. Many corporate managers and labor leaders are truly living in the past and are not recognizing the responsibilities of the present or of the future. But if we can successfully urge both management and labor to reflect on their present attitudes and why their relationship is so unproductive and how it is hurting our entire economy, perhaps we can break through to a mutually successful solution.

Remember the story about the scorpion and the frog?

There's a strong lesson there for management, labor, and all the rest of us. History demonstrates that those who do not change when circumstances urge change, do not survive. It's time for a change and it's time to remember the lessons of the past.

CHAPTER VI

THE NONUNION WORLD

"Less than 19 percent of the U.S. work force is unionized; more than 81 percent is not."

I t is truly amazing to me how people seem to equate the American work force with unionized labor. That is, of course, an unfortunate misconception. Less than 19 percent of the U.S. work force is unionized; more than 81 percent is not.

But it is safe to say that if organized labor is only the tip of the iceberg, as the tip goes so does the iceberg. Whatever happens above the surface also reverberates all the way down through the structure to its very depths. Employers of unorganized workers have recognized this over the last ten years and not only paid wages competitive with unionized scales but sometimes exceeded them. Much the same can be said of benefits and fringes, although parity is certainly not universal.

By mid-twentieth century the existence of a vast number of nonunionized workers resulted in the unionization of millions of employees. Unions were especially successful in their organizing efforts because management failed to treat its unorganized workers in a fair and equitable manner. This was very much the case from the 1930s through the 1950s as demands for security and a higher standard of living pushed American labor into the arms of unionism.

But beginning in the 1950s, and to a greater degree in the 1960s, management began to recognize that some of its policies helped to breed unionization. Through the 1960s the perception grew with both management and their employees that unions were indeed the vehicle by which workers could get wage and benefit increases. So management responded by meeting the competition. This had a dramatic impact, slowing down the growth of unionization and causing the number of union members to decline.

The offensive by nonunion employers caused unionized workers to take a second look at their own situations. They were paying hefty union dues in the 1960s while often nonunionized workers were getting paid as well as unionized workers without paying those union dues. The disenchantment of union members didn't happen overnight. In fact, it took at least a decade and a half for it to appear rather dramatically in data. But the data did show a definite uninterrupted decline in unionized workers as a percentage of the American labor force:

UNIONIZED LABOR'S SHARE
OF THE TOTAL LABOR FORCE

YEAR	TOTAL UNION MEMBERSHIP	UNION PERCENTAGE OF LABOR FORCE
1950	15.0 million	23.4
1960	18.1 million	25.1
1970	20.7 million	24.0
1980	20.1 million	23.0
1983	17.7 million	20.1
1984	17.3 million	18.8

Moreover, NLRB data shows an approximately 500 percent rise in the number of union decertifications for the decade 1965-75, reflecting the unhappiness of unionized workers with their union hierarchy.

But, whether unionized or nonunionized, it is important to realize that the worker of the 1950s through the early 1970s was quite different in outlook and personal convictions from his or her counterpart today. The employees of the 1980s are brighter, more sophisticated, more realistic, and certainly more independent. While this latest breed wants a competitive wage, and decent benefits and security, it is also concerned with how it is treated in the workplace. People expect work to be satisfying, interesting, and to have meaning. Motivated youngsters entering the labor force want to achieve distinction and self-esteem in the work place, not just earn money. More than ever before, matters such as communications and in-office or in-plant involvement and interaction are becoming strategic to successful labor relations. Employees of today demand jobs that satisfy not only the physical needs of the outer person, but the emotional needs of the inner person as well. Effective labor relations must deal with both facets of the modern worker.

There is, however, a greater difference between the workers of today and their earlier counterparts. Today's workers are burdened by more pressures than their predecessors. Employees today, for example, have a greater concern over job security because of the recent multi-year recession than had those of the 1960s and 1970s. Moreover, both management and workers alike are now forced to consider the issue of productivity more than in the past. And this poses an interesting, if not disturbing, question since, as the matter of productivity becomes more significant, the onus on the mediocre or less productive worker becomes greater and greater. That additional pressure also provides an open door for union organizing.

This is true because the majority of working America must fall into the less motivated category as its production rate indicates. Management, however, will certainly push for greater individual output, whether or not the economy continues to improve. The employees in the low to middle levels of productive ability, pressured not only by their bosses but by their peers, will only feel a growing sense of frustration. Fear will become the weapon that unions will wield in their organizing campaigns.

Managers of the 1980s and beyond will certainly realize that this new, growing perception of the pressure of productivity can only continue to create fear among employees. But there is a catch in what management can do with this knowledge. It certainly will not have the luxury or assurance that employees must produce to a certain level or be discharged. The labor market won't allow it.

There just may not be an adequate number of high quality, high producing employees to go around. It is already showing up in some fields. But in nonunion America, the average or less-than-average working group will be ripe for union organizing.

What is rather frightening at this stage is the fact that corporate America doesn't seem to recognize its responsibility to deal with these issues.

Most businesspeople remain so concerned with pure survival that they may continue to emphasize the wrong priorities. It isn't enough anymore to say, "We must be more productive." The issue really is "How can we become more productive?" The "how" can be attacked realistically by dealing with the fears and frustrations of the average employee. Employers must listen to them and accommodate their needs and anxieties. They must be spoken to, not commanded or patronized. In my experience, I find that about 10 percent of the working population consists of top-quality, hard-working individuals who produce satisfactorily. Because of their accomplishment, this 10 percent is generally more sympathetic to management. They seem to understand what must be done and how to do it. But we have also found that about the same percentage, 10 percent, are the lowest producers. They are particularly disappointed with themselves and their workplace, are frustrated and angry, and are almost always anti-management. That, of course, leaves about 80 percent of the working population, which may or may not meet productivity standards.

If management has any real hope of "buying these people off," it should quickly dispense with the idea. They are or will be union's meat unless management takes the initiative.

Taking Off the Blinders

A convalescent hospital in the Northeast provides a classic example of how not to treat employees.

The employees received wages and benefits which were certainly competitive to those of other employees doing similar work in the area. But a problem developed because the hospital administrator behaved like a tyrant. Actually a decent woman who worked hard and tried to do "the right thing," she acted like a horse with blinders. She simply wouldn't recognize that some of her activities were alienating employees. Many employees considered her unfair but could not get a hearing to voice their complaints. Naturally, this left a vacuum. The National Hospital Workers Union, through its Local 1199, tried to fill the void by organizing the workers. There was an additional dimension to the problem. The hospital's staff consisted of mostly Black and Hispanic women, while the hospital administrator and upper management were mostly white women. So racial antagonism was brewing there, too.

I tried to discuss with the administrator the employees' unfavorable perception of her. She always responded, "The employees are wrong." I tried to explain to her that the issue might not be one of reality but simply of employee perception, which could be changed. If she didn't change that perception, I warned her, the union would successfully organize the hospital's one hundred seventy-five employees. I analyzed where the hospital stood if an immediate election were to be held among the employees. My conclusion was that the hospital would lose by at least a five-to-one margin.

The administrator constantly told the employees what the hospital's rules were and how they would be enforced. She never asked the employees for input. Equally important, she had her "pets" and clearly played favorites among the employees. So it was obvious to me that the employees' negative perception of her was correct.

About a week before the scheduled NLRB-conducted election, it was clear what would happen unless something dramatic intervened. After I informed the hospital management of all the facts, it was decided to fire the administrator and replace her with the assistant administrator, who had a reputation as a fair person. I suggested a number of legal options and advised that she could address the employees, explain that there had been problems in the past, and *apologize* for them. I emphasize the term "apologize." The reason is that this presentation had to be a careful one since management cannot make promises to employees during an election campaign. Management couldn't, for example, make any promises that would specifically remedy the problems. So the thrust of the new administrator's presentation was that she should show the staff that she was an honest and fair individual who would try hard. In other words, it was on the order of "Give me a chance—and I will do my best to be fair."

The hospital won the election by ten votes. That was two years ago. The hospital is still nonunion and is being operated differently today than before. The new administrator has monthly meetings with the staff and more meetings when the need arises. She is very visible to the staff, always making herself available to all employees. She discusses issues openly and candidly.

In regard to productivity and work-load, the hospital's employees are continuously told that certain minimum standards must be maintained. I find that employees everywhere like to know where they stand at all times. In the case of the hospital, the administrator handles it diplomatically, telling the employees that if they have a problem performing their work according to the standards and rules, they should meet with their supervisor and discuss it. The goal, they are also told, is to try to maximize one's own potential, a goal that the hospital management heartily endorses. Several fail-safe approaches were built into the management-employee relationship. Each department supervisor holds meetings with her staff regularly, at least once a month. The employees are also independently counseled in a one-to-one setting at least every three months. And the supervisors have been coached to deal positively with employees and continually reward them by saying, for instance, "Thanks for doing a good job." These measures have been able to help the hospital's management to improve efficiency and productivity.

Other parts of the fail-safe program include quality circles and attitude discussions. At least once every six months each department goes through a quality circle program, adopting the routine which American business picked up from the Japanese. In this program, workers meet regularly to discuss improvement in product or service quality. The quality circle meetings at the hospital, lasting several hours, are intended to intensify employee involvement so that each employee understands that he or she has a role in improving the work environment. And at least once a year attitude questionnaires are distributed, seeking to learn from employees their true feelings on such basic matters as hours, wages, benefits, and working conditions.

Typical questions are: "Do you feel that you are being paid

fairly?" "Do you feel that you are being paid in a way comparable to other employees in the area doing similar work?" "If you were to receive other fringe benefits, list in order of their importance what benefits you would like to have." The result of both the quality circle discussions and the attitude surveys has been that management now has an accurate comprehension of the attitudes and desires of the workers as a group. It wouldn't be an exaggeration to say that they feel they are part of a big, happy family. And it was all due to the fact that the blinders were taken off.

How to Avoid the Unreality Trap

Picture this:

A substantial decline in the growth rate of the American labor force.

The need to consolidate facilities to remain competitive.

The massive shift in American industry from smokestack businesses to high-tech.

What does it all portend? Unions or no union, American management and labor will face declines both in the work force and in the basic manufacturing industries themselves. Without question, this is due to the continuing inroads of foreign competition which cause dislocations of human and industrial activity. But while America is losing its heavy industrial place on the world scene, its technological achievements in such dramatically burgeoning fields as computers, fiber optics, and genetic engineering will surely help her regain international superiority. Though this development will intensify, there will still remain many manufacturing businesses, reduced in scale and number certainly, but vigorous simply through determination and survival.

The challenge which faces us all should be treated as nothing less than a national imperative to become more competitive and more innovative and to recover our once high place in the world markets.

Two people well-known in their respective fields not long ago made pertinent comments: "The U.S. is at the eve of experiencing a substantial slowing in the growth rate of its labor force," stated Fabian Linden, director of consumer economics for the Conference Board, New York. Speaking before the House Task Force on Inflation, he continued:

> In the not too distant future, the working population will
> be expanding only about half as fast as in recent years. The
> difference between slow and rapid growth can have important
> and pervasive effects on the business environment of an era.
> For one thing, the size of the work force clearly has a lot to do
> with the pace of economic growth. For another, the relative
> availability of labor — as with all factors of production —
> eventually affects its cost, and that in turn has an influence
> on the level of capital investment. . . .

And John F. Welch, Jr., chairman and chief executive officer of
the General Electric Company, had this to say at the 1982 National
Association of Manufacturers' Congress of American Industry:

> Are we headed for what I call a quality recovery? By that, I
> mean a solid recovery bent on growth, but not just any kind of
> growth; growth based on investment. In other words, a
> recovery that has a major investment component in it to
> provide sustainable long-term gains for America in
> productivity and real incomes. . . .
> What frankly concerns me is what might occur in this
> '83–'84 recovery. Businessmen might feel very good from
> filling up relatively empty plants, leveraging the reduced cost
> base that we've all developed during the downturn, and
> building products in what are often relatively obsolete plants.
> True, in the short term, that will make our balance sheets
> a little healthier, our margins a little better, our bonuses a
> little higher. But by the end of the cycle, the country isn't
> any more productive than at the beginning. If that happens,
> we will have done nothing to really improve the underlying
> competitive position of U.S. industry. . . .
> If the quality recovery — a recovery based on investment —
> is our macro view of what constitutes a conceptually sound
> economic policy, then the micro view is where it really gets
> tested. . . . Just as important is a climate that allows business
> maximum flexibility in being competitive. If you have to
> modernize production to stay competitive — if you create

new factories in old shells— you may need fewer of them. So, in some of these businesses, we must continue to have the ability and flexibility to consolidate facilities. At the same time, we must recognize the pain dislocation creates and demonstrate compassion for the people and the communities involved.

A declining labor force and the need to become more competitive even if it means closing more factories and dropping more people means that a burden will be placed on both management and labor to be both pragmatic and yet creative in working toward a mutual goal. And that would be true of any national recovery above and beyond any bright blip in gross national product or industrial output. If one places the declining labor force and the need to become more competitive against the shift in the nation's economy from smokestack to high-tech activity, it becomes even clearer that the brains and imagination of everyone will be taxed to seek constructive ways of training and retraining millions of workers.

Given the problems it actually doesn't matter much whether we isolate the nonunion from the union sector. Although only 19 percent of the labor force is unionized, those workers have the same interests as nonunionized workers. The problems that exist in the nonunion sector are the same as those that management must confront in the unionized sector. The types of frustration and perceptions are generally the same in both groups of workers. To repeat, employers must realize that if the employee perception problem continues or gets worse, it will provide the unions with the rallying cry that made them so successful in the 1930s, 1940s, and most of the 1950s. That rallying cry, of course, would center on the claim that management fails to consider employee desires and mistreats workers so that unionism is the only recourse for employees. This development could easily offset the growing erosion in the ranks of unionized workers.

Enlightened management will make solving labor problems a high priority. If management accomplishes this and the economy continues to improve, it's likely that the number of unionized workers and their percentage in the labor force will continue to fall. As union members disappear, the very foundation of the union, its members' dues, begins to crumble. As this happens, unions will find themselves unable to afford union organizers to sustain the aggressiveness of labor in the field.

A large international union offers a case in point. I spoke recently to a former international representative who before serving in that post had been a field organizer for the union. He told me that he had been permanently laid off by the union along with about ten others who operated in the Northeast. Now in his middle thirties, this man had the reputation of being one of the more energetic field organizers in the area. But it didn't help him. He told me that as the union lays off its youngest, most effective organizers, the remaining union employees will be less effective in recruiting new members in the future. He said that the personnel who remained were generally older and hadn't had field experience for many years. Furthermore, he went on, those people would be generally unwilling to return to the field and live out of a suit case to do effective organizing. He also is convinced that even if they should go into the field, they most likely would not interact well with the newer, more independent employees who are not yet organized. If this example becomes typical — and indications at this point are that it will — it opens an opportunity for management to weaken labor's power base.

Within that situation lies a bit of irony, too.

Labor unions are suffering because of the nation's economic reverses, just as corporate America is. This has put the unions in the hypocritical situation of "Do as I say, not as I do." Labor itself isn't treating its own staffs as decently as it is insisting business should.

The harsh way that this particular union handles its organizing staff, the former field organizer said, was demonstrated in other ways. Not only was he terminated, but he was ordered to take his vacation earlier than he wanted. When he filed a grievance against the union, he was told in advance that he wouldn't "win" in the grievance procedure. If that is the case with this union, one of the biggest, how can organized labor legitimately suggest that it is the proper medium to protect workers employed by others? Whether or not this offers a strategy for management to combat unionism, it is certainly a development for unions themselves to ponder seriously. Cleaning up your own house is certainly necessary before you can urge better housework on others.

All in all, it's obvious that the nonunion sector, now running to about 85 million, will grow at a greater rate than will the unionized sector, even though there are growing signs that the total labor force will dwindle. This is happening because of the dwindling population rate, the increase in the number of professionals, the rise of migrant labor, and other reasons. But what will not go away is the urgency of building a better bridge not only to nonunionized workers but unionized workers as well.

CHAPTER VII

THE NEW FACE OF THE LABOR FORCE— OPPORTUNITIES AND DANGERS

"The advent of better educated, more sophisticated workers, more women, more blacks and youths with their sharpened motivation will unquestionably give our national skills a keener edge."

Yes, Times Have Changed

The low-slung, modern plant sits at the crossroads of two highways, some twelve miles outside the city's core. The beige-brick building, however, isn't very visible from the intersection. The choice of site guarantees easy access for its employees and the horde of trucks that brings raw materials and carries away the high-tech products made from them.

The wide variety of employees that staff its production and support activities surprise even the senior executives as they walk through the sprawling plant. They can hardly avoid thinking that times have changed.

Fifty-five percent of the staff is female. One woman moves her fingers deftly into a series of trays, places the pieces into an intricate machine, and sends the combined product on to the next woman. She works almost automatically and her thoughts drift to her family. Her husband, a blue-collar worker, will be the first to get home and will start preparing dinner for their two children. He has gotten used to it, as she has to her work at the plant. His income is limited by his occupation, but their needs grow with their children. She knows that she will have to continue to work and resolves to try to upgrade her specialty in order to earn more. Times have changed, not necessarily for the better, but at least she is helping boost the family income.

Fifteen percent of the staff is Black. One young man, moving constantly, walks along the rows of tables, checking the production flow. He is already in training for advancement, but it is none too soon. His father, a longtime porter in a steel plant which closed, has been reduced to catch-as-catch-can menial work. His mother still does housecleaning. He will have to improve their lot and his own. Loyal but clear-headed, he knows it is every man for himself. Times are changing and he must change with them.

An Hispanic youth, one of the 11.5 percent of his ethnic strain employed there, functions in a well-lit corner where his group receives the products combined and shaped for the final step in production. Although he hasn't completed his high school education, he is studying for his diploma at night. He is also engaged to be married and is extremely ambitious. He is one of six children, who together with their widowed mother form a struggling family. He and his mother, who works in a once large but now tiny sewing plant nearby, support the family. He knows that education and ambition are the two ingredients that will move him and his family upward. But how can he ever marry? He needs a break — no, an opportunity. It is a long way up from ground zero. He catches the smile of the young black nearby and they smile in agreement. Times have changed, man. Let's give them our own shot, the exchange implies.

In the rear stockroom a burly man in his middle fifties moves about with determination. He stacks heavy containers on pallets. He stops to run a heavy hand through his gray-flecked hair. One of the white male employees who compose 18.5 percent of the staff, he is bitter but realistic. He lost his job as a machine operator in a milling plant. He wasn't retrained because no one would hire him at his age for a job that requires years of training and skill, and so he compromised. No longer a union member, he is confused and annoyed, but never resigned. Times, yes, damn it, times have changed, but not for his benefit. He isn't that old that he couldn't have been retrained.

It is not, however, an unhappy plant. It is busy; there is a hopeful feeling because the company has been able to withstand the high-tech industry slowdown, and optimism prevails, corporately and individually. But problems hover outside the front door. Almost every day a station wagon pulls up before the plant and two union representatives distribute leaflets. The organizing drive is on. . . .

The New Numbers

In the Sunbelt states the face of labor has changed dramatically. There is now a rainbow of skin colors. Workers speak new languages and have different customs. In the Deep South the "good old boy" has been joined by many who lost their jobs in the industrial North, transporting new street-smart workers to that largely nonunion area. Blacks, Hispanics, Vietnamese, and other Orientals flow into Texas, New Mexico, Arizona, and Florida, competing with native southerners for jobs. Working women, increasing in number — one million a year — are becoming a new and independent factor in the labor force. The old mix, in which whites outnumbered nonwhites, is changing drastically. And the young, an increasingly more important part of the labor force, are more critical, questioning, and unattached than their elders.

In the factories, industrial parks, and other workplaces, the faces, the sex, and the age are hardly what they were a decade or two ago. Outsiders are often surprised these days by the people they find manning the assembly lines, machines, warehouses, and offices. In some plants, nonwhites already outnumber whites; women outnumber men; and teenagers and youths in their twenties outnumber those who are older. The mood too, is different. Reflecting their long climb out of obscurity, the new workers are more militant, less prone to unionism, more critical of management, less eager to accept the blandishments of either side or of anyone else.

Neither prosperity nor recession, war or peace, political ups or downs, appear to have materially affected the recycling of the American labor force. It has indeed changed, and changed permanently. Almost all trends showing shifts in types of workers, with very few exceptions, continue reflecting the sustained dynamics of the changing American work force.

The data are clear and revealing.

In 1954, white American women represented less than half the work force, 17.1 million in contrast to 36.6 million white males. But by 1976, they had virtually doubled to 34.1 million, while the number of males had risen about 40 percent, to 54.4 million. By 1981, there were 40.3 million white American women working, in contrast to 55.1 million white males. In other words, there were slightly more than four females working alongside of every 5½ males by the early 1980s.

Among Blacks, male workers rose 18.8 percent by 1981 to 5.73 million from 4.82 million in 1972. Black women's participation in the work force grew 38.5 percent by 1981, totaling 5.47 million, up from 3.95 million in 1972.

Hispanic workers also showed a dramatic gain. Their number jumped 76.3 percent from 1973 to 1981, from 3.46 million to 6.1 million.

The number of white teenage males in the work force increased enormously in recent years. Their number rose 131.6 percent, from 3.35 million in 1954 to 7.76 million in 1981. The number of Black teenagers in the work force grew 27.6 percent, from 8.78 million in 1972 to 11.2 million by 1981. While their increase was considerably less than that of white teenagers in that more recent span, it may be significant that their number by the early 1980s was about 3.5 million greater than their white counterparts. This may be explained, at least in part, by a greater need that is both economic and social in nature.

From the standpoint of all women in the work force, white and Black, the growth rate was 37.5 percent, from 33.3 million in 1972 to 45.8 million by 1981.

And in terms of teenagers, white or Black, the number grew 17.9 percent from 16.8 million in 1972 to 18.9 million in 1981. (See Table, page 95)

The growth in these sectors must be plotted against the

THE CHANGING AMERICAN LABOR FORCE

YEAR	WHITE MALES (16 & Up)	WHITE FEMALES	BLACK MALES	BLACK FEMALES	HISPANIC WORKERS	TEENAGERS WHITE	TEENAGERS BLACK
1981	55,045,000	40,365,000	5,731,000	5,476,000	6,107,000	7,761,000	11,207,000
1980	54,627,000	39,389,000	5,659,000	5,315,000	5,850,000	8,198,000	10,970,000
1979	54,130,000	38,665,000	5,579,000	5,189,000	5,304,000	8,509,000	10,767,000
1978	53,350,000	37,357,000	5,496,000	5,050,000	5,063,000	8,612,000	10,548,000
1977	52,547,000	35,615,000	5,340,000	4,801,000	4,676,000	8,406,000	10,141,000
1976	51,397,000	34,173,000	5,172,000	4,491,000	4,493,000	8,083,000	9,662,000
1975	50,409,000	32,839,000	5,022,000	4,305,000	4,233,000	7,875,000	9,327,000
1974	50,129,000	31,824,000	5,035,000	4,184,000	4,150,000	7,971,000	9,219,000
1973	49,953,000	30,756,000	4,997,000	4,108,000	3,463,000	7,833,000	9,108,000

expected slower growth of the American labor force, and what that portends for the new entrants of the 1980s. In the current decade, it's expected that the work force will add about 2 million as opposed to the 3 million entrants in the 1970s. This is due to the fact that the big gain in the work force resulting from the baby boom of the mid-1940s and 1950s is winding down.

There are 47.7 million women in the American work force already. The two-income family, more singles, and the need to keep up with inflation will all spur more women to either keep working or take jobs. Similarly, the increase in Blacks, Hispanics and Orientals entering the working ranks will continue to grow, not only because of economic reasons but also because of improving education, the demand for upward mobility, and growing immigration.

The U.S. labor force is expected to reach about 118.5 million by 1990, up from 92.6 million in 1975, the base year used by the Organization for Economic Cooperation and Development. This is a gain of 28 percent, well above Japan's 13 percent, West Germany's 4.9 percent, and France's 14 percent. Among democratic countries, with the exception of India, the U.S. will continue to have by far the largest labor force, about double the size of Japan's anticipated 58.9 million by 1990. Certainly the opportunities are vast if the quality of performance matches the increasing numbers. The example of what Japan has accomplished in regard to productivity and quality in the last two decades with a small but motivated work force is adequate proof that numbers alone aren't enough.

So much for the new multicolored, younger, increasingly female face of the U.S. labor force. Its new aspect raises a number of questions for management-labor policy and, more importantly, the quest for an improved industrial climate in this country.

What, for example, will the new larger force mean with regard to our ability to develop our national competitive ability?

How should the new workers be treated so as to improve our national productivity and to achieve a more cohesive business-labor relationship than we have had in the recent past?

How many will be unionized or remain unrepresented by unions?

Are both business and unionized labor realistic enough to recognize that the changed face of the labor force means that old policies may not work, probably won't work, and that new approaches will be necessary? Can everybody win?

The rest of this chapter will be devoted to probing those questions and suggesting some answers.

Coping Won't Be Easy, But There Are Ways

Unionized labor, in the form of the formidable AFL-CIO, was unsuccessful in its 1982 organizing drive in Houston and the Southwest generally. The drive failed only because the economy of the area turned sour, unemployment spiralled, and workers began feeling very insecure about their jobs. The weak economy left them cool to labor unions in the same way that it created problems for unions everywhere in the country.

The organizing drive led by the AFL-CIO's Lane Kirkland had seemed to make a lot of sense. In the 1970s new workers had poured into the South and Southwest from the depressed Midwest as well as from the Northeast. The lure, of course, was the boom in both the oil and construction industries, with high tech running a close third. In the early 1980s, the jobless rate in Houston, for example, was in the low single digits, whereas in the Midwest and some eastern states it was approaching double digits. The migration to the growing Sunbelt was understandably massive. Everyone felt that Texas, Florida, and contiguous states would continue to be the last to feel the impact of the recession of the 1980s, if they felt it at all. The unions were as convinced of this as anyone.

The Sunbelt held another attraction, particularly for unions. Many of the migrants who found jobs in the Sunbelt were midwesterners or northerners accustomed to unionism. Certainly management in the region, confident because of the right-to-work laws which made employment contracts illegal when conditioned on union membership, felt that labor unions didn't have a chance. Management may have been overconfident, the unions believed, since the labor mix had changed so much. It was one thing when workers at a particular Texas company were natives in a right-to-work state where unions were often equated with an evil force. But Kirkland, for one, was convinced that the odds were in his favor. And he could not, as a labor leader, ignore the southern population influx. But he did not apparently count on the combined effect of the nation's energy conservation drive and the general recession.

The organizing drive in the Sunbelt fell flat.

However, that was then and this is now.

As the economy continues to improve as it appears it will, unionized labor will know that it has a ready, if not willing, base in the Sunbelt on which to sustain a strong organizational effort. And it appears to me that management in the South and Southwest has so far failed to recognize this problem.

This was highlighted by an experience that I recently had at a nationally known Houston company.

At a meeting with eight of the company's executives, I made some recommendations to the president, who is a man of about seventy and a native southerner. When I finished, he turned to the others and asked, "Should we listen to this Yankee?"

The executives said nothing and after a few moments the silence became almost chilling. The president then began to smile and apologized to me. It was obvious why. He certainly must have recognized that seven of the eight were from the North. They were Yankees, too.

But that was just an example of regional prejudice, which I experience all the time. It represents a feeling of "I will do it my way and the best way is the old way." In my opinion, this dated, traditional thinking will certainly perpetuate the problems that must be eliminated. During the upcoming period of labor relations, particularly in the southern states, there will certainly be changes. They are inevitable. They must be made. I question, however, whether there will be enough time to make the necessary changes before the labor unions run wild in the South.

There is also the matter of companies pulling up stakes in the North and moving to the South. There have certainly been actual cases of "runaway" companies. But the perception of businesses "running" to the South in order to avoid their obligations to labor unions only increases the determination of unions to mount offensives in the South. The perception goes even beyond unions and amounts to a conviction that running to the South is an effort to avoid obligations to *all* employees, whether they are for or against unionism. If this perception remains or grows, workers in the South, whether born there or not, will scarcely be inclined to trust management. Faced by a credibility gap, management will continue to have the problem of having its motives continuously under scrutiny.

The problem grows in scope as one realizes that the new face of the American labor force, whether in the South or the North, consists of an unprecedented number of Blacks, Hispanics, women, and others. Several of these groups, including Blacks and Hispanics, have long felt that they have been mistreated by white corporate America. Women for decades have fought against inequities in employment and salary. How can management win the trust and confidence of this new labor force?

Fair and candid communications are at least a good beginning to solving the credibility problem. If, let's say, management decides to move from the North to the South, or anywhere else, doesn't it have an obligation to the old as well as the new employees to explain clearly why the move was made? Don't employees deserve to know? Of course they do. If management is straightforward in dealing with the perception that it is "running away," it can nip the credibility problem in the bud and begin building some real employee support and motivation. Candid talk is the way to start a program of productive give-and-take and mutual consideration.

The two-way exchange proved pivotal, although tardy, in relation to the problem at an Atlanta hospital several years ago. The employees were being organized by an independent union led by a Black pastor, who was both a political and racial leader in the community. This union had successfully petitioned the NLRB to hold a representation election, and a date had been set.

I was brought into the case about two weeks before the election. The problem was simple, but management couldn't see it. Most of the hospital's employees were Black, with the women outnumbering the men. The male employees were almost exclusively Black. While some members of management were Black, the three highest-ranking executives were white, but this was not the real problem. The hot issue seemed to be pay and benefits. But as in many other cases, the real problem was one of management's attitude toward its employees and the impact that attitude had on the perceptions of the employees. This was the case even though some of the other local hospitals paid their employees more. The workers at the hospital in question had repeatedly asked management why their wages were lower than wages at other facilities, but the hospital brass never answered them directly. Usually they responded by giving the employees an embarrassingly low wage increase. This not only perpetuated the wage-and-benefit differential but increased the workers' sense of unfair treatment.

These hospital workers had really been sitting ducks for a labor union organizer for some years. Before the latest incident the Laborers' Union had tried to organize them. Those organizers were mostly white. When the heads of the Laborers' Union told the workers that there was no justification for the wage and benefits gap, many employees didn't fully believe or understand. They felt that the white labor leaders may have conspired with the white management at the hospital.

But when the new union organized under the direction of Black leaders whose numbers included a pastor, whatever was now said about the wage-and-benefit differential was understood and *believed.* There was very little that could be done in the two weeks before the votes were cast. I did succeed in reducing the union margin, but the union prevailed.

The election was not the end of this story. I was asked to negotiate the contract for the hospital. I learned that the reason for the wage-benefit gap was that the other hospitals were larger, had some private paying patients, had larger outpatient clinics, and had more sophisticated equipment, such as advanced X-ray facilities, which supported bigger profit margins. Some of the other hospitals also had certain specialties such as a psychiatric outpatient clinic. All of these, of course, contributed to bigger profits at the other hospitals, enabling them to pay their employees more money. I saw also that the hospital I represented was inefficiently managed, overstaffed and truly unable to pay more than it was paying.

I met with the Black union leaders and laid out all these facts and also showed them the financial statements that I had obtained. Once I was able to convince them that the problem at the hospital was not basically one of mistreatment but perhaps just of failing to communicate the real facts to the employees, I was able to obtain a written contract that afforded the employees a nominal increase. Even though the hospital remains unionized, the employees, after getting all the real facts, feel closer to management than they ever have and are better motivated.

When management began breaking down the barriers, the employees saw them for the first time as "a decent bunch." The workers then shared suggestions with management about how it could operate more effectively. Employees made suggestions about overstaffing and how the hospital might get more efficient use out of the staff. And there's the irony. If management had realized some of the mistakes that it was making before the organizational campaign began, I truly believe that the hospital would be nonunion today.

But if Blacks present a difficult challenge as they become a more important factor in the American labor force, it is my opinion that women will present the most serious challenge. Women today want to share in the educational and vocational wealth of America. They reject the old stereotypes that relegated them to a limited number of jobs with little room for promotion and leadership roles. Conscious of past and present mistreatment, women are apt to be militant and ever conscious of their newfound strength and independence.

Some unions have tried to exploit past inequities to gain members, even when the inequities have been fully redressed. But it is possible to cope with this tactic, as we demonstrated when we were retained recently by one of the nation's largest insurance companies. An organizational drive was then being orchestrated by a "Working Women" organization called District 925, which had affiliated with the Service Employees International Union. The focus of the appeal during the organizing drive was women's rights. The rallying cry was that white, male corporate America had been abusing women for a long time.

However, the insurance company was able to successfully defend itself against District 925, and quickly enough so that the union was not able to get enough support even for an election.

The insurance company was successful because it had already involved its female supervisors in management decision-making.

Management also made women's rights a consideration in many policy-making decisions. Top executives met regularly with the employees to build an employee-involvement program. The company was fortunate. Its management had been progressive enough to have already instituted some form of employee-involvement activity, but that program was neither implemented effectively nor conducted on a sufficiently regular basis. The company, however, was especially fortunate that the union had mounted its offensive early enough for management to react. They were able to nip the problems in the bud during the skirmish of the war.

If the union had been more alert, it would have waited to "instigate," so as to soften up the employees for its approach before it came stomping across the horizon.

Public pressure groups such as "Working Women" or the NAACP intensify the perception that certain types of employees have long been mistreated. The proselytizing of these groups has helped to convince many employees that they are indeed bright and independent. Whether everyone might agree with that or not doesn't matter as much as the fact that these employees do perceive that they are bright and independent. This being the case, the burden falls upon management to make these workers feel that they certainly aren't being mistreated and that they are — or will be — involved in the decision-making process.

An identical burden also falls upon unions as well as management. If women workers have a dominant or growing sense of their independence, organized labor must understand that and deal with it. If labor fails to deal effectively with that sense of independence, it may find that the changing makeup of its members will mean that it will be unable to control its membership. I am concerned about this because I do not see labor doing its job well in this area.

But involvement in decision-making isn't really enough. Management and labor must realize that the new workers are better educated than their predecessors. High school graduates now fill most entry level jobs and a full quarter of the U.S. labor force has completed at least four years of college. They have high expectations regarding the conditions and rewards of work. They are more "tuned in" to issues, human rights in particular, than their counterparts of earlier years. So it's too simplistic to say that these better educated workers are primarily interested in having management involve them in a general sense in decision making or that the company should take great steps to ensure that past discrimination isn't perpetuated. We assume initially that smart management will do these things.

The real test of bright corporate management in the future will be its ability to be sensitive to some of the specific issues that the new work force considers paramount. These issues will include on-the-job training or retraining; providing opportunities for upward mobility through outside educational subsidy; equitable or fair handling of the age issue, whether it involves the older or the young workers; and, in fact, the handling of employees in a manner that takes into account their special needs in terms of sex, age, and family condition.

This brings us face-to-face with a paradox — the opposing needs of the new, younger workers and those of the older ones. The workers, ages eighteen to twenty-five, insist that their job rights be balanced with the older workers, ages forty to seventy. The older employees don't want to be shunted aside because of the demands of youth. It's a Catch-22 situation. And because of this "youth versus age" dilemma and the frustrations it causes, both groups are becoming increasingly prone to unionization. The pulsing core of the dilemma is job insecurity.

Ironically, protection for the older group has aroused fears in the younger group. Federal law protects employees in the forty-to-seventy year bracket. Hence, if layoffs should occur, the younger employees fear that they will be the first to go. From a legal standpoint, they may be right. Increasingly there is litigation concerning "reverse discrimination" although its import remains unclear. There's no certainty how this litigation will evolve, but it's safe to say that generally the protected groups will continue to be protected.

Although there is no easy answer to this apparently no-win situation, management has to remain sensitive to the problem. We tend to minimize the issue when the economy is running strong, but it becomes sticky in a weak economy when business pulls in its reins and cuts its operations. Recent court decisions are taking into account the new face of the labor force. One such ruling which was later reversed held that layoffs on the basis of strict seniority are invalid if they create a disparate impact because too large a percentage of Blacks, women, minorities, or other protected class members are affected. The intricacies of the problem therefore increase. Management may feel it has to protect the older workers, but it may not be able to do so in a particular situation if the vast majority of younger employees are Blacks. No one, as a result, knows what to do.

Involving the employees, inviting their reactions and suggestions, can offer a solution.

In a recent case, when I served as a management-labor consultant to a Fortune 100 energy company, a layoff plan was formulated which both complied with the law and was based on both skill and ability. Seniority, or age, was a factor. But it was only one factor among several. The program suceeded because management was smart enough to invite employees to submit ideas about how workers should be treated. This created a feeling among the company's workers throughout the U.S. that management was trying to develop a fair system that would be good for the company and *fair* to all employees. Incidentally, that took enlightened thinking on the part of both the company and the workers.

In this chapter, we have been concentrating on the burden the new work force places on management. But labor, as we have said, has not responded sufficiently. If unions continue to fail their responsibility in this connection, we will certainly see more disputes and strikes in the next few years. Inevitably labor will find more confrontations within its own ranks, wildcat strikes and other disputes caused by the insurgent "new majority." Such new forces have a tendency to throw out or leave the incumbent union and form a new, more liberal, even more militant union. This is hardly a fiction. District 925, mentioned earlier, a union of mostly women, is an example.

If all these things take the direction already indicated, management's problems could become almost insurmountable. Not only will management have to deal with problems as they relate to employees in general; they will have to deal, too, with problems caused by special interest groups. We may begin to see in the labor movement some frightening developments: a force of women fighting men, Blacks against Whites, young against old — all pushing for favorable position and priority in treatment. The social strife involving Black rioting in the 1960s could look like a Sunday school picnic compared to what may lie ahead for the rest of the 1980s and the 1990s. The development of self-interested factions within the labor force could mean more militant action in other ways. With women increasingly becoming a significant part of the work force, a strong majority or a silent minority could rise in protest of either management or the incumbent union and could conceivably reach out to a new union like District 925 for help.

Let's return to the questions posed earlier which were raised by the new face of the American labor force.

What will the new work force mean with regard to our ability to develop our national competitive economic and commercial clout? My opinion is that the advent of better educated, more sophisticated workers, more women, Blacks, and youths with their sharpened motivation, will unquestionably give our national skills a keener edge, a hunger that we have lacked in the recent past. But, conversely, their special demands will require both business and labor to rise to greater heights of understanding, sensitivity, and wisdom in order to produce a working harmony. This will be absolutely vital in terms of our ability to compete with the success of the world's great exporting countries.

How should the new workers be treated so as to improve our national productivity and to achieve a more cohesive business-labor relationship? They must be shown that both business and labor intend to treat them fairly. They must be shown the possibility to grow in a job. There must be open communications and incentives in terms of both earnings and opportunities for personal recognition. Obviously, the fragmented nature of the work force makes all this difficult. But, the opportunities that arise from sensible, even wise, treatment of employees are well worth any such efforts. Can the special groups submerge their own interests for the general good? That will take the best talent that the leadership in business and labor can summon. But what is the greatest competitive asset that American business has? People, obviously. So efforts to engender a strong esprit de corps must command the top priority.

Nonunion corporate America might well consider having peer reviews — that is, having employees participate in grievance committees consisting of, say, three members of management and two employees. Such a committee should rotate every month or so to change this ratio and employees elected to the committee should be changed every month. Employees on such a committee not only would give it balance, one that would change to draw more workers into it as it is rotated, but would also have the effect of judging peers by peers. I have found that employees put in a judgmental position tend to be tough on other employees who are lagging or misbehaving. The reason for this toughness is that the other employees are inconvenienced or have to work harder because of the misconduct of a few.

How many employees can be unionized or remain unrepresented by unions? It's obvious that unions won't stand still for the decline in their ranks and, despite such disappointments as the lagging organizing drive in Texas, will push ahead with new drives. Hence, it's reasonable that there will be some recovery in their numbers. Whether the gain in pure numbers will show a recovery in the unionized share of the increasing labor force appears questionable. The question is whether special groups will see enough gain in joining the national unions rather than going it alone.

Are both business and unionized labor realistic enough to recognize that the changed face of the labor force means that old policies cannot work and that new approaches will be demanded?

That's the big one, the key question. Probing that question is the purpose of this book. We believe that it is certainly in the cards for both management and labor to rise to the occasion. The issues, brought into precise focus by the new labor force, are very clear. What is needed is a sense of realism and pragmatism. And a sense of urgency.

We need to be realistic and move quickly because the changed work force is fraught with both opportunities and dangers. It is a two-edged sword that must be wielded properly or it can cut dangerously.

As the labor force continues to shift and take on new dimensions, the challenges will grow. Given the shifts in their demands and resulting frustrations, it is not inconceivable that a corporate society of employees could emerge — workers owning businesses. This is already portended in the rank and file buy-out of the A&P stores in the Philadelphia area and similar developments in some of the midwestern industrial states. It would be a third segment in our management-labor society, a hybrid, with some clusters of workers forcing entrepreneurism in order to build their own destinies on the ashes of bankrupt companies.

If employee companies should spread well beyond the present small number, a workers' corporate society could be an important new contender facing both business and labor.

PART TWO

THE
VITAL
NEW DIRECTION

CHAPTER VIII

NEEDED: A CONTINUITY FOR COURAGE

"A coal miner for some fourteen years, Eddie observed, 'Sometimes I sympathize with the companies.' "

Wisps of Change?

An improving economy heralded good times as the mid-1980s approached. A sense of anticipation gripped the nation.

In the media, questions were being asked, interpretations attempted, suggestions volunteered. The American economy had narrowly escaped disaster. Somehow, the mechanism which bound the national economy together had started functioning again. The nation breathed a sigh of relief, but the fears of economic disaster weren't entirely overcome. Something was still obviously grating in the very guts of the economy. I couldn't help thinking that with the respite we had gotten it was time for some honesty, some hard-nosed realism. It was time to brush away the old "we/they" blinders.

If there was any new aspect in the relationship between American management and American labor, it was plainly an inching, a straining, toward some sort of rapport. The recession and the consequent rise in the joblessness had sapped both sides, and when the jobless rate fell, both sides had reason to ponder. The petulant rhetoric persisted, but it had lost its sting.

Labor and management, traditional opponents, weren't quite ready to sit down with each other as partners, but each seemed to feel that they could no longer afford to be enemies. Labor gains had been scaled down; strikes weren't as bitter as they had been a year or two earlier; there was an increased acceptance of arbitration.

It was obvious that times were changing — and quickly.

In the coal town of Carmichaels, Pennsylvania, the closing of the Robena Mine, once the largest in the world, cost another six hundred sixty coal workers their jobs. According to one newspaper account, Paul and Eddie Blandish, father and son coal miners, had sharply different opinions about the closing and who was to blame for it.

A coal miner for some fourteen years, Eddie observed, "Sometimes, I sympathize with the companies. There have been times when the union has gotten out of line by asking for too much."

His son's words fell on the ears of Paul Blandish, fifty-six, as if they were blasphemy. As president of his local union of the United Mine Workers of America, the older Blandish had seen membership drop from 9,000 to 3,400 workers, yet he remained a hard-liner and urged a tougher line on contract talks. "I'd be willing to say 'no way' on any concessions," Paul asserted. But at the same time he bemoaned the fact that he could not get his sons or other young men to be active in the union. "I tell them: Come to the meetings; get involved. Hell, I'd step down anytime for a younger man. But it seems they just don't care."

Victor Riesel, the labor columnist, took occasion to note that General Motors' return to profitability meant that the world's biggest automaker would begin sharing its profits with its employees for the first time in its history under a special profit sharing plan. He added, too, that "GM expects sufficient black ink flow to provide $12 million a year to innovate free legal services of many kinds to its UAW members."

As if this development weren't enough good news, the AFL-CIO's executive council called for a national industrial policy in which labor would join business and government in modernizing older basic industries and developing technologically advanced new industries. But while the council welcomed the lower unemployment rate, it noted that millions were still without jobs or had only part-time work and that the number of Americans now at the official poverty-line levels had risen to almost 15 percent of the country's population.

Still there were signs that management and labor were beginning, just beginning, to get together. Referring to a settlement reached between American Telephone and Telegraph Company and the Communications Workers, *Industry Week* observed: "It [the settlement] clamps a lid on costs but bends enough to please the union. 'Nobody left the room complaining,' reports one inside observer."

And in Pittsburgh, as *Industry Week* further noted, a proposed employee-buyout of a National Steel mill in Weirton, West Virginia, by some 8,000 union members will not only be the nation's largest employee stock ownership plan (ESOP) "but may also become a model on how to optimize for success."

A Partnership That Works

If the time is right, if the changes in attitude and outlook are proper and if the economic circumstances are favorable, what can be done? A scenario for a new relationship between American management and labor is essential. The catalyst will be a new, working partnership. Dynamism between the two partners will be needed to make that partnership work.

Signs of a new attitude on the part of both management and labor surfaced during the two day, professional baseball players' strike in August, 1985. As the grumbling public began to wonder whether it should write off the second half of the season and, perhaps, major league baseball in its entirety, both the owners and the players compromised and the strike ended abruptly. The owners gave way on the free-agent re-entry system, which players disliked, and on the free-agent compensation system (the principal issue in the 50 day strike four years earlier). The players also made concessions, agreeing that eligibility for salary arbitration be extended from two to three years.

Kent Tekulve, the Philadelphia Phillies' relief pitcher and player representative, called the settlement "a fair one for both players and owners."

"I don't believe negotiations are supposed to be won or lost," he told the Philadelphia *Inquirer.* "Negotiations are held to get an agreement that everyone can live with. You don't go in there to win or lose. You go in there to come up with a deal. So, in that sense, we both won."

* * *

In the first half of this book, I showed that the old adversarial arrangement between management and labor didn't work, and the problems which that failure created. Now, in the second half, I will spell out a vital, new direction. The program will be laid out in brief in this chapter and elaborated in much greater detail in the next five chapters.

1. Business and labor must adopt new criteria in dealing with one another. The adversarial relationship which has existed for so many decades has produced distrust. Because the relationship has lasted so long and appears to be endemic, it poisons the working relationship between management and labor. In the last few decades unions have competed with management and with other unions in a game of one-upmanship. The game proceeds in this manner: Whatever the contract was three years ago, claims the union, isn't as good as it has to be now. If one union in an industry obtained a better contract, then another labor union will try to do one better for its employees. This creates an endless cycle, creating an inflationary spiral and a fantastic perception by union members that anything goes.

Embroiled in the inherent distrust and faced by the inflationary spiral, management invariably attacks the union demands with the response, "I can't afford it." The strange thing is that both sides knew that they were sending out false signals. Management decided early in the game that it would adopt a hard stance to match labor's inflexible posturing. Coming at the onset of negotiations, management's hard stance only stiffened labor's back. The union hasn't helped matters, by asking for the sun, the moon, the stars, which in turn stiffened management's resolve to hang tough.

Despite management's position, the unions were almost always able during the 1950s, 1960s, and 1970s to push their demands through. What emerged from this pattern was a tradition of distrust and a credibility problem. Labor-management negotiations often boiled down to a brutish animosity. Lack of credibility and posturing rather than negotiating were most evident in the strike of the United Auto Workers against the International Harvester Company in 1980. This strike so clobbered the company that it was almost driven out of business.

Looking back with the benefit of hindsight, the sequence of events is all too clear. It would be comic, if it wasn't so sad. The union made outrageous economic demands. The company said it would never accept them. The union struck for months. When the strike ended, management agreed to almost all of the demands. The damage to International Harvester was irreparable. Obviously, both sides indulged themselves. Distrust, an absence of credibility, and muscle-flexing hurt them both.

The Harvester situation is very similar to the one that faced many other companies in the same period. But a strange thing happened. Even though in many strikes it was clear that the company was convinced that it could not agree totally with the union's initial demands, in most cases the employees did well by striking. Employees came to believe that they would always win if they struck. Even in cases where the employees lost out in a strike, the perception in the workplace was that the union and the employees "won" the strike. This perception, in fact, was not realistic. Unhappily, this problem was exacerbated by headlines which focused on how much the employees got in the new contract. Relegated far down in the story — or not mentioned at all — was what the employees lost while striking and what the company lost during the work stoppage.

Obviously, the "old ways" have failed us. International Harvester is dramatic proof that the old ways no longer work. The company today has some of the highest-paid unemployed workers in the world. Those workers can hardly derive any pleasure or solace from the knowledge of their past high earning power. The example shows that not only do employees lose but management also loses under the old ways. Other once powerful companies such as Braniff Airlines and Wilson Foods were hurt by strict adherence to traditional ways of dealing with labor, and labor was hurt by dealing in its characteristic adversarial way with business.

One of the major reasons for this destructive management-labor tug-of-war has been the very nature of the way big business has dealt with unions. Big business, which has been behind the major industrial growth of our society since World War II, made the mistake of entering into multi-plant and multi-employer collective bargaining agreements. Both big business and "big labor" probably even today could easily rationalize adherence to this policy on the ground that it minimizes the cost of collective bargaining. In other words, instead of negotiating fifty or one hundred separate contracts, only one need be negotiated. For business, multi-employer or multi-plant contracts were the easy way out. They gave labor the upper hand. It was a very inequitable arrangement.

Why did collective bargaining involving more than one employer give the unions the advantage?

The answer is simple. A strike during that type of bargaining process could, and often did, bring down the entire business or major segments of an industry. We have seen this in such industries as transportation, steel, rubber, and automotive manufacturing. Industry-wide bargaining added to the power base already established by big labor. We saw that in the trucking industry major strikes can't be successfully endured — or, for that matter, won — by management. Independent companies can easily fill the void in the marketplace. When the United Auto Workers struck American manufacturers, foreign competitors leaped into the breach. This can happen in any company or industry which is stalled by a strike and is in a market that can be plugged by smaller independents or foreign producers.

What is needed to correct all this is a new sense of reality when management deals with labor. Both business and workers are locked in a struggle which transcends their old adversarial relationship and which requires a joint front against the erosion of productivity. The need for management-labor cooperation demands an end to traditional muscle-flexing which hurts everyone and a reordering of old priorities which have made American industry a weak competitor internationally.

2. Business must adopt new criteria and make new judgments. Unlike management in such other countries as West Germany, England, France, Italy, and Japan, American management has generally refused to allow its workers any voice in making decisions of policy or strategy. Businessmen, regardless of the size of their companies, have behaved like the aristocrats of another century. Indeed, within their own executive structures and within their own plants, the "haves" have stubbornly refused to give leeway to the "have nots." After the worst recession in decades, the raw reality is that the great majority of businessmen have scarcely learned that they have a mutuality of objectives with those on their payrolls. Little wonder, then, that eroding worker motivation has contributed to lagging productivity and declining quality or workmanship. Such results have widened the door to foreign imports.

None of this is new. Many know it, but few have taken steps to correct a situation that will simply fester and worsen.

The problem is clearly self-perpetuating. The tougher and more indifferent managers are to employees, the more intransigent and resentful the employees become. Somewhere along the line someone forgot to extend a friendly hand and the alienation of employees spread across the entire terrain of management-labor dealing.

There are exceptions, of course, where management has shown a more enlightened course. At M.H. Lamston, Inc., a New York-based chain of variety stores, at least three barely profitable stores of the thirty-two store chain are kept alive in order to train managers and give younger people a chance to move up. United States Shoe Corporation, in St. Louis, a company which has generated a much admired acquisition policy allowing it to diversify broadly out of the shoe business, says it has found that new ventures create excitement and improve morale among its employees. And there are other examples of enlightened management.

Broadly speaking, business seems to recognize its obligations to its workers only when a crisis develops. Usually that recognition comes when a company's fortune lags, when it is about to be struck, or when union organizers knock on nonunion doors. One company distributed this memo to supervisors as it sought to repel a successful attack from a union:

> Our company is committed to preserving our supervisors'
> and employees' rights to deal directly with each other rather
> than through a third party. . . . Every department within the
> company is a potential target for union organizational activity.
> Professional union organizers do not pick their targets at
> random. They concentrate their efforts in areas where they

believe they have a reasonable chance for success. Frequently, unions are contacted by dissatisfied employees who believe they have a problem or concern that has not been handled properly by management. Employees will not normally seek out a union if they honestly believe management tries to understand and address their individual problems and will continue to do so in the future.

Each supervisor either has or will complete the "Quality in the Work Place" training program. Here are some basic refresher points from those and other sessions which all supervisors should remember when dealing with the employees they supervise:

Make yourself available. Handle all complaints quickly. Be a good listener. Communicate clearly. Give your employees a feeling of accomplishment. Keep employees informed.

Much of the foregoing is admirable, although it is patently an effort by that company, a Midwest manufacturer, to defend itself from union organization by taking the initiative with its employees. The intent is spelled out in the memo's introduction: "The company is proud of its commitment to positive employee relations and the work environment we have developed. Our personnel policies and programs are designed to ensure that employees will not feel the necessity for organized or outside representation. We strongly believe that neither unionization, or other third party intervention, is in the best interest of our employees or the company." Very often the best defense is a strong offense, and in taking this kind of initiative, companies often are able to set the tone for the kind of positive employee relations which keep a plant running union-free.

Maybe so. Maybe not. *The way in which the company actually treats its employees, rather than the instructions it gives to supervisors, is what really counts.* No one is asking that the company give away or subjugate its profit goals. But unless the same unhappy adversarial relationship is to continue with labor, business must adopt a new, enlightened attitude toward its workers and implement it in meaningful ways. Better communications, more candidness, greater consideration, and a sensitivity to individual needs are basic requirements. Management must improve its training procedures.

3. Labor must defuse its internal political problems. If unions are to deal with management on a realistic basis, they must first get their own act together. They must stop breeding adversarial attitudes within their own ranks, between local unions, and between industry-wide unions seeking to encroach upon each other. While problems have developed in those three areas, the most important one requiring remedial effort is the first in which internal strife prompts a militant stance toward management and results in unrealistic demands on business. Very often, union heads striving to counteract threats to their leadership from opposing members tend to overcompensate when they deal with management. They know they are overreaching in most cases. But this is a ploy to quell the budding militancy of a new faction within the union ranks. In trying to solve a minor problem the local union leaders create a greater one.

What could be less constructive or productive?

As has been pointed out earlier, union rigidity has been not only self-defeating because it has meant lost jobs, but also it has resulted in a decrease of information given to union members. It does not matter whether union leaders see more rank and file involvement as a threat to the union hierarchy or whether there is an inherent structural deficiency in unions. What matters is that in significant ways the behavior of unions has been as damaging as the behavior of management. The time is long gone when either side can justifiably claim that it is the other side which has been the sole villain.

In the local union halls, a new era of democracy must begin in a first strategic move toward more useful and pragmatic dealings with management.

Rank and file should be told of the true situation about an employer's ability to meet new wage demands and whether he really needs concessions from the union.

Politics within the local must not be allowed to set the amounts of those demands but should be geared to ensure that leadership, policy, enforcement, bargaining, solicitation, and general procedures represent the viewpoint of the majority.

Younger people on the union rolls want to be heard,

especially if their attitudes differ from those at the top, and they should be allowed to speak up. Without their voice, the union movement, as the Robena Mine incident shows, will definitely atrophy.

Similarly, the new members of the organized labor force — women, Blacks, Hispanics — have to be recognized, their needs attended to, and their voices, too, allowed to be heard. Unless unions give careful consideration to their wants, unions will continue to reflect the old-time thinking and the nonproductive ways which, in fact, represent less and less of the attitude and needs of the current union movement.

The next phase of the transformation of unions as they come to grips with reality is the need to stop raiding rival union locals, rival industry-wide unions, and rival unions representing different fields. Unions have always been eager to invade each other's territory. Any management foolish enough to foster this internecine warfare will soon regret it because any new union is unlikely to be more democratic or more reasonable than the predecessor. And any union leadership which is intrigued by the greener-looking grass is likely to be disappointed by the problems it inherits as a result of its foray into some other union's territory.

Unions, as stated earlier, are up against declining membership, diminished credibility, and internal strife. A new threat, conglomerates seeking to coordinate all of their divisions' offensives against unions, has already raised labor's hackles. Will that be the wave of the future? Litton Industries, one of the nation's toughest multi-industry companies, is carrying on such a fight, despite some fifty citations for unfair labor practices issued by the NLRB. This coordinated offensive, new in the management-labor field, prompted Howard Samuel, an executive of the AFL-CIO, to assert bitterly, "Relationships between unions and management are at an all-time low."

Needless to say, the pressure is on. Unionized labor must get its house in order by defusing its internal politics and adopting a much more democratic order.

4. The challenge of job security must be attacked head-on. Job security is one of the trickiest, most complex issues in view of the loss of several hundred thousand jobs during the recent three-year recession. Jobs *are* being eliminated and many workers are panicking. Workers direct their disenchantment at both the employer and labor unions in equal measure. Many workers are convinced that both have led them down a double-dealing and double-talking path. Moreover, as I have shown in Chapter II, the concessions reluctantly granted by workers in the interest of job security have generally not led to that goal.

Against this background, there's no doubt that resentment and fears involving job security have heightened the adversarial relationship. For many decades workers carped, complained, fretted about their employers, but in their viscera almost all of them bore the certainty that somehow the owner-manager would protect their jobs. This belief lay at the root of the employer-worker equation; now that basic assurance has disappeared, leaving millions of workers feeling helpless and angry.

The harsh reality is that no company or institution can any longer guarantee job protection. Industry dislocations, the unending rise of imports, and economic recessions preclude any such guarantees. The solution lies in training, in preparation, and in continuing reorientation and communications. Both management and labor are obligated to work independently and collectively to develop training programs to deal with new automation, with robotics, and needless to say, with retraining in the event of plant transfers.

The training and retraining of workers can be one of the toughest hurdles in achieving a much more harmonious management-labor environment, but in today's new realities it isn't an impossible one.

5. Top Priority: Reeducation of employees. What has been the effect of "big labor" on "big business"? When big labor wields its power unwisely by exacting contracts at almost any cost, big business reels from the blow so that a major element in our industrial society almost collapses. Big business in a great sense spawned big labor by agreeing to company-wide collective bargaining. But when labor won what it demanded, it made such domestic industries as automobile manufacturing unable to compete with the Japanese industry. The Japanese used that opportunity to eat into the American automobile market and eventually to take a big bite out of it.

Unfortunately, most experts believe that the American auto industry will never regain the part of its market that it lost to the Japanese and the Germans. What this means to our society and to the labor unions is that fewer Americans will have jobs and fewer workers will remain union members. One would think that this would be an easy conclusion for unions to reach. But the sad part about it is that unions can't or won't understand or believe this reality, or simply can't accept it.

The typical union attitude is something I have run into many times but never more dramatically than on two television programs in which I participated in 1983.

On one, in March, on a program called "New York, New York," Frank Barbero, New York State assemblyman and chairman of its labor subcommittee, declared that management was wrong, morally and otherwise, to use "union busters." He flatly predicted that the adversarial relationship would continue indefinitely. It seemed to me at the time that Barbero, however well-intentioned, was a throwback to the Great Depression, the bad times between management and labor.

In May, the same year, on the Phil Donahue show, I was involved in a debate with Sandy Pulaski, an executive of the United Electrical Workers Union. Management, she insisted, acts irresponsibly and treats workers unfairly. It seemed to me that Ms. Pulaski's adversarial thinking was probably more appropriate for the 1940s and 1950s than the 1980s. I found the audience reaction surprising, however. Despite the harsh realities of the very difficult recession, the audience appeared to be almost equally divided between management and labor.

While there were, perhaps, more management supporters in the Donahue audience on that particular showing than there would have been five or ten years ago, I would have thought that the large number of unemployed Americans might have caused more people in the audience to come out against organized labor. The core of the reactions of the Donahue show audience, I realized later, was emotional. I think that this might be our real problem. The audience was doing more than simply expressing opinion. Those expressing pro-management sentiment were bitter in their opposition to those who came out in favor of labor. And the same vociferous feelings and comments came from those who sided with labor against management. It was a good deal more than a debate. The intellectual, practical, and even realistic aspects of the issues in the debate were clearly lost in the heat of emotion.

Why do we have to look at labor and management, at what they are doing and what they stand for, as either good or bad? Isn't there a middle ground? The experience of the Donahue show is simply more evidence that most of America has neither found nor understood the middle ground or the need for it. We must somehow establish the need for a middle ground through an educational process. If unions are unable to deal with this problem because of their own political problems, then a successful educational campaign through middle America can work to make the hierarchy of the labor movement more responsible and willing to deal more effectively with reality. I sincerely believe that this political problem — labor leaders feeling that they must look good in order to be reelected, no matter what the cost — can only be circumvented by a successful educational campaign directed toward working America.

By focusing on reality and practicality, I believe that the solutions to problems can be achieved. In other words, will labor leaders sacrifice their own positions and their political lives in order to help the future members of working America? It's doubtful. But if the rank and file becomes still more knowledgable, more practical, and more realistic through this educational process, then sometime in the future it may be easier for union leaders to respond more constructively and effectively to the joint problems of management and labor.

Management, too, must educate itself more about the people who work for it. It must concentrate more on changing employee attitudes. It should focus more clearly on the difference between perception and reality. Management can no longer assume the traditional paternalistic approach and say, "You'll do it my way whether you like it or not because I know what's best for you." Management, however, can assist in the educational program by making efforts to involve employees in the decision-making process and by developing more and better benefit programs relating to up-to-date employee interests.

6. Better productivity or robotics? In the quest for a more realistic attitude toward each other, management and labor must foster and inculcate the need for increased productivity in the plant, the assembly-line, the worker, and the man-hour level. This paramount necessity will solve many problems and will add a solid floor to the overall challenge of generating greater management-labor harmony.

Business will then have the ability to obtain a better, more economic yield while achieving greater competitive strength. Business will also be able to cope with any unions which remain incalcitrant or seek excessive gains. Increased productivity will benefit unions by making their internal politics easier to handle and by facilitating dealings with management. The unions themselves will be more effective and young people therefore will have a greater incentive.

These developments are occurring against a background of robotics, the technology that is gradually appearing in more and more assembly lines to replace blue-collar workers. In Japan and other countries use of robot machines has become commonplace and is revolutionizing industrial techniques. In the U.S. the greatest strides in robotics have been made in the automotive, household-durables, and semiconductor manufacturing fields. But we are way behind other countries in this field.

Retraining workers displaced by robotics will be a major concern. But without a new scenario to improve plant productivity, the U.S. will find itself more at the mercy of foreign producers. The solution lies in joint efforts of both American management and labor to combat this threat.

7. Government involvement must be more judicious and objective. There are two phases to government as a factor in management-labor relations. One is already in operation and the other which should be studied is the introduction of a new arbiter agency or commission.

The National Labor Relations Board must become more objective and redefine its goals. It must give up its participation in areas in which it has no real influence, skills, or historic success. The best example is in the bargaining process when the NLRB is asked to interpret whether the employer has made a "fair" offer. The record shows that all we can expect in such cases when interpretations are made is the interjection of a biased sensitivity. Both management and labor have sharply criticized the NLRB for the agony they felt was caused by idiosyncratic judgments.

Earlier I cited a recommendation that a new government agency be created to deal with situations in which conflict is likely to lead to bitter or protracted strikes. I also recommended the use of a special Presidential commission and/or Congressional commission to develop such an agency so that the political process might be eliminated as much as possible in formulating the agency.

A Federal agency empowered to step in at the right juncture and with the proper skills could well avoid much of the pain and dislocation caused by may of our recent strikes.

How would such a new Federal agency work? It might be envisioned as an expanded Federal Mediation and Conciliation Service. The difference would be that the new agency would consist of representatives from outside the government as well as inside, representing both management and labor. It would have the immediate or emergency power to settle strikes and solve labor disputes. For example, when an employer wants to close a plant and relocate because a union is unwilling to make the necessary concessions, the new agency might be armed with the power to maintain the status quo for a short period until solutions are found. It really doesn't matter at that "put on hold" phase who is right or wrong. Closing a plant or moving might be a tragic mistake, while finding an alternative solution might prevent one.

The new agency power would resemble the President's use of a 180-day cooling off period. But a hold period of that duration would not be necessary because in most instances a decision should be forthcoming much more quickly. A thirty-day cooling off period might suffice.

8. Clearing the air with new semantics. There's no doubt that specific words or terms in management-labor dealings often raise red flags and needlessly create controversy. Both sides know it, yet both indulge in wars of words as much to impress colleagues as to foolishly maintain a traditional offensive in order to send the opponent back on his heels. The value of continuing this is very questionable.

If it is true that "a soft word turneth away wrath," it is likewise true that soft words only work if both sides use them. Is "grievance" more apt than "problem-solving"; or "we/they" more apt than "team" or "all of us"; or "conflict" more apt than "problem"? Obviously not. But will management or labor use the better expression for fear of seeming too conciliatory? Obviously not. So it's clear that if we really expect a new semantics of harmony to replace the old, failed semantics of conflict, its use must be mutual.

The technique, if properly applied, goes well beyond making a "confrontation" into a "discussion." Semantics only reflects the thinking process and attitude of those who speak. At the Nissan plant in Tennessee, the Japanese automaker doesn't call its employees by that name but rather refers to them as "technicians"; likewise, its managers are referred to as "planners" or "expediters." And the technicians, by the way, wear "work apparel," not uniforms. All of that patently is done to eliminate as much as possible the "we/they" attitude.

Beyond that, it's essential that the one speaking must understand some of the basic tenets of communications. It is important to realize that communicating is a two-way, not a one-way, process. The speaker must be assured that the other or others are in fact listening and hearing and that he or she is indeed also listening and hearing when the other's turn comes. Moreover, the communications process can be affected by the speaker's style. The listener can't be made to feel that the speaker is talking down to him or her.

The plain fact is that the hard-nosed approach on both sides has created and led to the use of overfamiliar trite terms which both sides in fact know are nothing but the tired terms of the same old confrontation. Let's take an example. Normally, the union negotiators during the actual negotiation process submit their laundry list of "demands." The very word "demand" starts the negotiations on an adversarial note. It implies competition, hostility, conflict, "we/they." Then, the union puts the employer on the defensive by discussing its "grievances." Management, on the other hand, starts off with comments about "tough times," or "difficult competition," or "those damned imports." It's all a sort of game designed to get the opponent off balance.

But wouldn't it be better if the union started off by making a request for items which management considers to be possible changes to the existing collective bargaining agreement? If the process had begun that way, it would immediately permit management to discuss matters in a cooperative way with a greater possibility of achieving resolutions that are more team-oriented than confrontational. Does this approach give management an opportunity to moan and groan? Of course. But if management takes that course rather than make the obvious effort to cooperate, the negotiations will be unproductive and sterile from the outset, which is certainly foolish — and self-defeating — for management.

What is really needed, of course, is very evident. One can hardly adopt a new, more realistic, more pragmatic attitude without couching it all in terms of cooperation and conciliation. But, as we have stressed throughout, a change in attitude must come first. It has often been said that "actions speak louder than words." But the right words and expressions can do a great deal to smooth the way.

9. Stop using the media for effect. Americans should have become inured, if not cynical, to all the propagandistic statements, charges, and claims of management and labor about each other. The U.S. Chamber of Commerce charges the NLRB with an antibusiness stance and releases a seventy-three-page document to support its allegations. The unions belabor management. Management strikes out at unions. The media jump on it all, responding to the size and hyperbole of the vituperative blasts.

Individually or collectively, management and labor must stop using the media as a vehicle for adversary activities. The results are harmful, often to both sides, posturing for the media arouses more resentment and builds controversies. Sometimes the effect hurts individuals, even those who are well-meaning. Take the use of the media when the AFL-CIO called management-labor attorneys "union busters." This created the perception that any attorney or management consultant was a union buster because that individual worked with management. The problem lies, of course, in the power of the headline and in the superficial reading habits of most Americans. They tend to read the headline and the first or second paragraph, ignoring the body of the story, which usually gives the perspective and the nuances.

Public perception is certainly a key ingredient in the total concept of a greater harmony between employers and employees. One can only hope that the public will get so satiated with the verbal crossfire that the exercise will surely be counterproductive. That is to say not that muzzles should be applied to either side, only that caution, wisdom, and discipline should be brought to bear on public utterances.

10. Bargaining: Honest and realistic or face-saving and hostile? By now it should have become obvious that American management can no longer conduct its bargaining with labor as it did from the 1950s through the early 1980s. During that long span, business gave away more than it could afford and in effect mortgaged its future. By the same token, if unions proved to be intractable, some of the fault lies not only with the lack of communications between management and union leadership but between the latter and the workers on the union rolls.

But now we are reaping the inevitable result of that harsh confrontation. If management finds that it has to bear the brunt of a strike, it does so. That is what Continental Airlines, Master Chef, and Greyhound did, knowing fully the difficult path they were choosing. But in the eyes of their management, it was the only course left to them after difficult dealing with labor.

I have had dozens of conversations with union leaders in which joint management-labor problems were discussed. I am constantly being told privately that labor may be amenable to some type of cooperation with management as long as the solution makes labor look good. The very heart of the collective bargaining process is an extension of this as the weeks and months of talks drone on. Even after months of negotiations, management may make a final offer without calling it that. This is a signal to the union official sitting across the table to follow through with a prearranged, off-the-record private meeting and/or agreement. But that isn't the end of the charade.

The union official then knows that he or she will return to the bargaining table after a caucus and protest loudly and then present the union's final position. That final position is often just a token request for some small additional item to settle the contract. This is nothing more than a face-saving gesture so that the union leadership looks good to its constituency.

This is just as true in the grievance process as it is in collective bargaining. In cases when employees are fired, the union official in a private meeting will ask for reinstatement but without payment of back wages. The so-called "deal" seems to be an integral part in the labor relations process. Labor leaders think this is necessary for their survival and the rank and file has become accustomed to labor "winning." But all this does is add to the adversarial process while hoodwinking union members. Joint management-labor committees charged with the responsibility of defining how business and unions can coexist more constructively may help to remove many of the unnecessary, time-wasting steps in the bargaining process. The joint committees could also serve another purpose. They could thrash out issues in a closed advisory meeting. They would thus be in a position to influence leadership on both sides for the resolution of many matters without recourse to animosity or charade.

What is needed, it seems clear, is an entire change in the process and attitude as management sits with labor to thrash out a new contract.

"Thrash out." No more. That's the old, nonproductive way.

"Resolve problems" is a much better way of putting it.

CHAPTER IX

FOR BUSINESS: NEW CRITERIA AND NEW JUDGMENTS

"Thus, one of big business's prime tasks will be to find ways of crossing these communication barriers."

Turning the Tide

Tension had taken over in the Chicago plant. There were three pressure points. The employees on the assembly line were troubled. The plant manager's face was taut. The Teamster organizers outside the iron fence were determined. The emotions that crackled to and from all three points had quickly polarized into a potentially explosive state.

The situation wasn't world-shaking. It was, after all, taking place only in one of several plants belonging to a manufacturing company which was part of a division of a conglomerate. The local press had given it only token coverage. The conglomerate's management paid little attention, considering it entirely the division's responsibility. The division considered it the responsibility of the company. The parent, a national firm on the Fortune 100 list of biggest companies, was just too big to worry about a plant flare-up.

Convinced that he had it all under control, the plant manager was cool on the outside, but not on the inside. Young, only a few years out of business school, he had served little time in the trenches. He knew that the only way to handle employees, even those being courted by a union, was to take a hard line. Quite naturally, the workers were annoyed by his haughty pronouncements, tough orders, harsh decisions. Yet in one informal caucus after another they hesitated to vote the Teamsters in. It was hard, disturbing, to rend the fabric of the private world that they and their fathers had lived in all those years.

Yet it was only a matter of time, perhaps only days. Unlike the conglomerate's management, the company's president, agonizing in his office just a few miles away, realized that things were going badly. Unless checked, he believed, the union drive might even lead to total organization of his other plants. He couldn't just sit by and let that happen.

One morning he appeared at the plant and told the manager that he would personally talk to the workers. He held a number of informal "roll up the sleeves" meetings with them. The result was a series of revelations to the employees. They soon realized that even though mistakes can be made on a local level, the real policies were made at the upper corporate levels. They saw for the first time that the people up there, as represented by the earnest president, were indeed human.

Patiently, candidly, he discussed with them the variety of problems that he had to face in his decision-making capacity. And they began to see that the company president was apparently as concerned about job security, human aspirations, and the economic fears of the employees as they were themselves.

It turned the tide.

If the American economy is to be maintained with big business as its pacesetter, big business must take a step back and learn from its past mistakes. If management does this, one of the first questions it must ask itself is "How will the new work force view the new management?"

Broadly speaking, corporate America today is being run by professional managers who in the main are graduates of business schools and have more book knowledge than their predecessors. Whether realistically or not, employees view the new professional managers as totally bottom-line-oriented individuals, conscience-less and inhuman supervisors. Thus, one of big business's prime tasks will be to find ways of crossing communications barriers so that it can understand itself better and improve its perception among those who work for it.

As the above real-life incident shows, the communications barriers can be crossed. Traditionally, however, upper management throughout the rarified corporate stratosphere fails to involve itself at the lower levels. Apparently, the senior managers feel that if they meddle in the company's local problems, they would be "dirty-ing their hands." Of course, we have to be realistic. The president of a major or even medium-sized company can't spend a lot of his time traveling from plant to plant. But the need for a new climate in labor relations requires more involvement by upper management in human and labor relations.

As I have already said, employees nowadays insist on more information coming from the senior management. It's vital, too, that this information be consistent from the highest to the lowest levels of the corporation. This is not always the case, and that is usually the fault of upper management. That is as much as error of commission as it is of ommission.

What's behind this failure in communication? The reality is that every level of a company tries to carve out its own kingdom. A plant is the kingdom of the plant manager; a district is the kingdom of the district manager; the regional manager is king of all he surveys; and so on. The inevitable results are abuses. Rules within a company must be fair. If they are applied consistently, issues like "mistreatment" or "inequities" will fade away. I have several times stressed in this book that employee attitudes about how fairly they are treated are among the most important factors influencing management-labor relations.

How to Hire Productively and Start Right

You run a company that doesn't need much direct supervision and so it must have self-starters. What do you do? Hire what you think are the best candidates and let the best and the brightest even-tually rise to the surface like so many corks? Forget it. Not today when businesses more than ever before need competitive clout. Loyal employees who don't have to be told what to do every minute make all the difference. I have a story to tell about the hiring process, another key element affecting labor relations.

Traditionally, the interviewing of new employees is conducted in an unprofessional and unscientific manner. If a company has three interviewers, each inevitably has his own way of doing things. This leads not only to unscientific evaluation but to poor judgment as well. If an upper manager is trying to judge the credentials of three applicants and if the interviewers asked each applicant different questions, what standards will the manager use to rate the applicants against one another? In that sort of situation it isn't difficult for the manager to make mistakes.

There's another way to do it.

In a project that our firm had with a large Fortune 500 company, the objective was to analyze the applicants from the standpoint of their attitudes and to develop a profile of the people that the company should be seeking. This could be strategic. Suppose, for example, you are dealing with a company which, because of the type of jobs involved, won't have a lot of immediate, direct supervision. The people to be hired may need the ability to be self-starters. In other jobs the ability to be a self-starter may be detrimental. If that ability isn't needed for the particular job, the person with that trait may quickly become frustrated and thus increasingly nonproductive.

After completing the profile, we developed questions that every interviewer should ask each applicant. Next, after consulting with industrial psychologists, we developed a range of responses to the questions. These responses were grouped into both positive and negative responses and compared to the profile, which contained both negative and positive characteristics. If the profile included twenty positive and twenty negative characteristics, and if twenty questions were posed to each applicant, we could then objectively rate each potential employee. And if each correct answer were given one point, it's easy to see that if twenty questions were asked and the maximum score were twenty, one could, for example, receive twelve positive points compared to eight negative points. If this was compared to another applicant who received eighteen positive to two negative points, the selection process becomes much easier.

After the selection, the employee is monitored for the first thirty days and then evaluated sixty days later. Evaluation and rating forms are given to supervisors to allow them to grade the employee. By doing so, we found that employees improperly hired could be weeded out quickly. After using this system for this particular company, we found that of the first one hundred new employees hired, only two mistakes were made. We also found that this new work force was performing two to three times the work that the company projected. In fact, the company had originally anticipated that it would have to hire at least two or three times — and possibly four times — as many employees as it eventually hired to do the necessary work.

What was significant in this program — and I believe it can be for others as well — is that the education process was initiated when the applicant was interviewed rather than after being hired. It should be noted, too, that people were selected for the job interviews after prescreening. Prospective employees were asked to write why they felt that they could perform a particular job after reading the job skills listed in newspaper advertisements. As each applicant was selected, the interviewer was prepared to explain what the company was all about, its policies and philosophy. A policy statement was furnished to each interviewer, who gave a copy of it to the applicant. The policy statement said in essence that the company believed that a one-to-one relationship in dealing with the employee was its very cornerstone.

Was that antiunion? No! But it was a defensive measure. The company wanted to remain nonunion and sincerely believed that it didn't need any outsiders to help it maintain a good relationship with employees.

After being hired, the new employees underwent detailed orientation. They were given all the rules and regulations and the reasons for them. A slide presentation followed. Since the company wanted to remain nonunion, the presentation explained why it felt that unions weren't necessary for its employees. In it, the salient labor issues were openly and honestly discussed. Interestingly, of the several hundred employees hired to date under this new process, only one voiced any criticism about the slide presentation. Regardless of a particular company's perspective, it's important to be open and candid with new employees and to launch the communications process at the earliest possible time.

With this particular model as an example, there is a clear direction which corporate America can take. It is axiomatic that you can have the best selection process in the world, but if management at any level is inferior or simply untrained in the human labor relations area, the best of company programs, its best intentions, and its most sincere communications policy will just fail. Good will alone won't make it.

Managers Are Trainable, Too

Imagine starting a training session by attacking top management. What seems heresy actually worked because it loosened inhibitions and aroused the participants to express their feelings about the company and about those above and below them. And it really cleared the air.

Initially the foregoing project led to the development of a thirteen-week training program for managers. The resulting program proved to be very unusual because it included managers from the lowest level to the highest levels in the various group sessions.

At first the upper managers attending the meetings felt that the training programs were beneath them. It was practically an insult for them to be present. Conversely, lower management was flattered to be in a training session with the upper level but also felt fearful that something that one of its members might say would be held against him. In the early sessions the upper management people appeared to be sleeping, while the lower level managers were conspicuously silent. I had to work my tail off in order to maintain a reasonable energy level among the participants.

To make the meetings successful, I had to openly start attacking upper management. For example, I would ask the upper managers whether they really understood their own labor relations policies. Eventually I got some of them to say, "What policies?" We then discussed other sensitive issues such as their knowledge or lack of knowledge of employees. Sooner or later they admitted that they didn't know the employees below them very well. Even that wasn't enough to break the ice. But it finally happened when one of the lower-level managers told his boss that he was "full of shit" after the boss uttered some ridiculous platitudes. The lower-level guy further told his boss, "You don't know what you're saying. You don't even know anything about me or what I do." After some prodding, the boss admitted that the lower-level supervisor was right.

Those were some of the approaches taken during the thirteen-week training program. Each meeting had its own subject, such as communications, grievance-handling, and so on. But the real thrust of the weekly meetings involved human interrelations and interaction. From those meetings, management drew several conclusions.

The first was if management didn't continually follow-up on each other and with the employees by reinforcing positively whatever had been done, the internal communications effort would surely fail. Another conclusion was that a committee within the management group should meet regularly at least once a month to monitor problems and problem-solving techniques in the company or plant. Without this type of follow-up, there could be no consistency in managerial communications or any real interaction with employees.

After the committee on management began its meetings, one person was selected in each management group to act as a buffer or liaison with the other management groups. This was to solve problems which might occur if, for example, a particular supervisor at one level found it difficult to apply a certain rule or standard to his employees. In order to maintain consistency, it was agreed that supervisors would clear the problem and work out a solution through the management liaison representative. Even though it was concluded that the supervisor might "violate the rules," the decision and the reasons for it were communicated to all the other managers. In many such cases, the reasons for solving the inconsistency were communicated to the employees as well.

Obviously, the refinement of these techniques established solid foundations for building trust among managers and between managers and workers.

Dealing with People: Talking Straight, Understanding, Caring

A major American corporation recently told its dealers: "Regardless of company size, the spirit of your company is shaped by the people you choose as employees; your employees affirm what your company really believes, really wants, really stands for. They speak louder than words and tell a clearer story than any figures. Are you spending your 'people dollars' wisely?"

For those companies whose managements do not yet realize

it, traditional communications techniques do not work anymore. Employees are getting smart. They know nowadays that much of what management tells them is only what it wants them to hear. Employees consider the rhetoric contained in company newsletters, newspapers, and magazines as propaganda. Often, the bigger the company the worse the employees regard its efforts at communications. Size of a company, however, is no real criterion for judging the quality of its communications. The quality of its communications depends on how enlightened and how considerate management is. And that can come in companies of any size.

Some companies are making honest and sincere efforts to communicate effectively. I have already discussed such things as group meetings with supervisors and middle management on a monthly or bi-monthly basis and meetings two or three times a year with members of upper or middle management, such as plant managers. Other traditional communications methods are memoranda to employees or other publications that are posted on bulletin boards or circulated as newsletters. Picnics, Christmas parties, and Thanksgiving or Christmas gifts of turkeys or other items are also traditional ways of making contact with employees. But the real keys to the right kind of communications which can go much beyond traditional methods can be broken into two categories: real interaction between management and employees; and involvement in the decision-making process.

Interaction between management and employees requires some fundamental techniques and approaches which might initially seem simplistic. One basic approach calls for training supervisors to understand those who work for them. Most lower-level supervisors have a great deal of pressure imposed upon them to "produce." While producing is important, it can hardly be done without the sincere help of employees and a mutual feeling of cooperation. The "I can't do it without your help" ingredient must be communicated by the supervisor to the employees. It may seem ridiculous but training programs on how to teach supervisors to accomplish this, even how to say "thank you," are sometimes necessary.

One of the things that I have learned and taught managers is how to profile the employees who work for them. It's actually a simple, non-threatening approach to improve labor relations. I have had each supervisor meet with employees on a periodic basis to develop data on how they are doing from both professional and personal standpoints. On a personal basis, each supervisor should know whether or not an employee has children and possibly even their birth dates. These little details become important in establishing sound interpersonal relationships. A supervisor can set up a tickler file and be reminded that an employee's child has a birthday coming up. On that day he can either send a card to the family or to the child and/or congratulate the parent-employee. Each year this is done reinforces the relationship.

Much the same pertains to periodic employee evaluations. Many times employees only know when they do things wrong and rarely hear when they do things right. As opposed to the normal evaluation sessions where the employee is told how he or she is doing, I believe that supervisors must be trained to recognize the need to tell employees not just how they are doing but how they can do it better. This will not only aid their relationship but certainly improve productivity. It's fairly easy to utilize this process to its optimum. "Joe," the supervisor could say, "I know that you have the stuff to do a better job than you are now doing." If he can suggest how, it will work even better. Supervisors somehow do not approach a problem involving an employee in that way. Typically, they say: "Joe, you aren't doing a very good job," or "Joe, things aren't working out like we hoped." Or "Joe, you're doing a fair job but we think it ought to be better."

The opportunity to go beyond such criticism to gain an improved performance while still making the employee feel he is respected is just lost.

Top management has a tendency to blame its lower-level management when there is a feeling of negativism in the work force. But it's really the upper management which should be blamed because it often fails to train its lower-ranking executives effectively in the art of human relationships.

One way in which employers can involve employees in the process of decision-making is through the use of quality circles; gathering employees to discuss performance and quality of product. Quality circles can involve employees in real issues such as productivity, downtime, coffee breaks, pension needs, staff-scheduling and so on. Much can come out of it, depending upon the supervisor's management skills and his understanding of employees. Employees, too, must be encouraged to participate actively in such exercises without turning them into gripe sessions. What's important here is the tone that the company and the supervisors set for the discussion. Most employees will see the discussion as an effort to involve them further in the workings of the company and to remove their instinctive distrust of management and its motives.

How involved in the company should workers be? Consider the following philosophical statement made by the president of a large Japanese auto parts manufacturer: "The work should be there for the benefit of the worker." The implication of this statement is that workers should feel vitally involved with the product and the company. Employers should fight against the "we/they" attitude, communicate effectively with employees, and strive to have employees identify their interests with those of the company, not some other organization.

What to Do If the Unions Don't Go Along

Certainly, if many of the above suggestions are taken seriously by management, real strides will be made toward a more harmonious and productive relationship.

Obviously, given the intentions behind these efforts, it's neither good logic nor common sense for unions to balk. But, just as obviously, if business management begins to do all the "right" things for employees, there's a strong likelihood that employees will realize that unions may be unnecessary. The fact of the matter is that if unions see this happening, they are probably right to worry about it.

Can the problem be circumvented by involving unions in management policy and strategic planning? It may sound great in theory, but it's difficult to see how that could work in the real world. What, for example, can a union hierarchy do if it participates with management in the establishment of a new policy and the rank and file workers for whatever reason don't go along? One way that this can be avoided is for management to discuss new or significant changes in policy with the union leadership to determine whether that policy would have any significant impact on the employees.

One catch is that if management does its job well, there will be a definite attitudinal change among the rank and file. Another catch is that if there is such a change, the unions will fight the situation all the way. But despite these two catches, management will win out by doing its job properly.

The implications of this push-pull problem are long-term. Even though many employees now out of jobs blame the unions at least in part for their problems, certainly at least 50 percent of organized workers are still militantly, even blindly, supportive of their unions. The implicit confusion within the unions can sometimes produce ridiculous tragic events. On April 6, 1983, in Pittsburgh, President Reagan was greeted at the airport by angry steelworkers who *en masse* shouted obscenities and blame at the President. There was a harsh irony to that mass protest by unemployed workers. He was in the city to attend a retraining conference, one that might prove to be the real salvation of the protestors themselves. The real issue is how to make those protestors, and other union members who are bitter, understand what is needed. Yet it is hard to escape the fact that as long as a sizable portion of the working public, employed or unemployed, feels so desperate, fighting on the streets remains a real possibility.

Some good signs are emerging, however. Members of the United Food and Commercial Workers Union, who were quite bitter when A&P closed its stores in Philadelphia, turned their anxiety and anger into entrepreneurship. Some of these workers, with the support of the union, headed by Wendall Young, are now running several of the supermarkets abandoned by A&P. Such cases enable the working public to understand the types of problems faced by management in the marketplace. Running a business that survives can't be a one-way street either for management or the unionized workers. Both have a responsibility for its survival. Workers just can't expect an automatic wage increase every year without corresponding increases in such areas as productivity and the benefits of economy of scale.

What if the union hierarchy doesn't cooperate?

Management really has no choice but to talk straight to employees. Open, honest communications which lead to involvement of employees in all aspects of the business are vital. Putting a worker in the boss's chair in order to explain the heart of a problem may be difficult to swallow, but it's a pill that will cure the illness. In so many industries, management will simply have to get across to employees that the recent recession and those which came before it have created a new direction not only for the company but also for their industry. It's all part of the education necessary for the working public to understand that American business is deeply involved in a fight for life.

The domestic steel industry unfortunately offers a classic example of how not to do it. Conversely we may learn from it how to do better in the future. Steelmakers agreed to take some savings and reinvest them back into the industry. Whether the reinvestment was done politically as a face-saving gesture for the Steelworkers Union is probably beside the point. The fact of the matter is that the steel industry in the United States as we know it will never return. Unless the steel industry seeks new directions such as diversification into other fields, the steel companies will probably never regain the top competitive position which they once enjoyed in the international marketplace. How can they if their costs are too high and their operating economics are way out of line compared with companies in other countries?

Thus, the very agreement which was last negotiated in the industry simply set a moribund foundation from which only chaos could follow. Steelworkers, many of whom voted to ratify the pact because they just didn't know any better, now feel that they were fooled. Evidently the Steelworkers' Union is not taking the blame, especially as 1983 ended and U.S. Steel, the industry leader, announced new, severe plant closings and cutbacks. In interviews and letters to newspapers, we constantly read that steelworkers complain that management "screwed us." They are right, but only in part. Both management and unions were equally culpable.

As a matter of fact, it may have been better, more sensible, and more realistic for the steel industry to liquidate many of its plants, take the savings that were created, and reinvest them than to try to build a foundation upon a lie, as it did. Both management and the union should have entered into an agreement that unemployed steelworkers would have the first crack at new jobs in plants opened by companies currently in the steel industry, even if those plants operated in other industries. Union members might well have bought that proposal. What they got instead, because of the long-standing adversarial relationship between management and labor, was a general acceptance of an unsavory scheme as the only way to buy everyone out.

The situation then, was the very reverse of talking straight to employees or union members, both from the standpoints of the company and the union hierarchy.

One thing we have learned during periods of national crises is that Americans know how to take it and to rally when tough situations develop. We are in such a situation now and absolutely must involve our working men and women in the fight to improve productivity and to give our industry the will to compete better.

Management, too, must take a deep breath, get rid of its old fear of working people, and reach out to them in meaningful ways. Actions speak louder than words, of course. But even the right words, if honest and candid, will be a good start.

CHAPTER X

FOR LABOR: A PARTNERSHIP RATHER THAN AN ADVERSARIAL ROLE

"The bald fact is that organized labor cannot survive unless it adopts new attitudes."

A Close Call

On February 22, 1984, American labor, already sorely beset by the continuing erosion of its membership and persistent pressure to grant further concessions, received perhaps the biggest jolt of all. The Supreme Court ruled unanimously that filing for bankruptcy could free a company from its union contracts without being required to prove that the company would fail without obtaining such relief.

It was a double-edged sword.

It cut against labor because any company which decided to avail itself of the voluntary Chapter XI proceedings of the Bankruptcy Code could summarily cancel its union contract even before receiving court permission to do so. The obligation to honor an agreement signed between management and labor was deemed subservient to the Bankruptcy Code's intent to provide "a debtor-in-possession some flexibility and breathing space," according to the Supreme Court's finding.

The other thrust against labor came in the form of a provision in the ruling which stated that before granting a company's release from its labor contracts, the bankruptcy court should assure itself that the company has made "reasonable efforts" to work out "a voluntary modification with its unions."

An employer, then, could void a union contract if he obtained court protection under the Bankruptcy Code, even if he wasn't about to go down the drain. Under the "voluntary modification" ruling, unions had to make concessions or face contract abrogation if the employer decided to go into bankruptcy.

Thus, the court decision struck at the soft underbelly of labor's anatomy. If concessions so desperately sought by business weren't working, if unions were beginning to stiffen their backs when business demanded that they give up previous gains, the Supreme Court's dictum bypassed all the rebuttals that labor could possibly summon up. Even without claiming imminent failure, a company could demand concessions. If the company didn't get them, the company deciding to resort to Chapter XI could cancel its labor agreement, whether or not a threat of imminent failure existed.

Predictably, labor screamed. Ironically, this bad news for labor occurred during the annual meeting of the executive council of the AFL-CIO at Bal Harbour, Florida, and quickly became a hot subject of discussion among the five hundred in attendance.

"We're disappointed in the decision," said Lane Kirkland, president of the AFL-CIO. "We'll pursue a legislative remedy in the Congress." William Winpisinger, president of the International Association of Machinists, called the court decision "outrageous. This was never the intent of Congress." Henry Duffy, president of the Air Line Pilots Association, said he was "deeply troubled" by the ruling. Laurence Gold, AFL-CIO special counsel, told the New York *Times* that the Supreme Court decision "obviously enhances the opportunity for union-busting techniques." The labor movement was working vigorously with Congress to secure amendments to the bankruptcy laws, he said, which will "prevent this kind of manipulation of collective bargaining agreements." The court ruling will obviously be a spur to the labor movement's efforts, Gold said.

Long-standing Federal laws had, until then, barred the overturning of collective bargaining agreements in the railroad industry, said Gold, and "what we want is an overall rule similar to the rule governing railroads and railroad unions." He added: "There have been many successful railroad reorganizations even though employers are not allowed to overturn and tear up collective bargaining agreements in that industry."

The court decision resulted from a 1980 bankruptcy filing by the Bildisco Manufacturing Company, a building supply company in New Jersey. The company had failed to pay a scheduled wage increase after filing for bankruptcy status. Eight months later it received court approval to terminate the union contract. When the International Brotherhood of Teamsters complained to the National Labor Relations Board, the NLRB ruled that the unilateral decision not to pay the wage increase was an unfair labor practice. But a Court of Appeals refused to endorse the agency's ruling.

The case then went before the Supreme Court under a joint Teamsters and NLRB appeal, but the high court agreed with the appeals court. It was a stunning setback for labor.

Seen almost from any standpoint, the surprising Supreme Court ruling reinforced the growing use of the bankruptcy statute by companies that weren't insolvent to cut their unionized labor costs. In 1983, both Continental Air Lines and the Wilson Food Corporation canceled bargaining agreements as part of their petitions for court protection from their creditors under the Chapter XI umbrella.

The stunning labor upset naturally brought an excited flow of articles, letters, and editorials in the nation's press. As both management and labor organizations continued to lobby Congress, the coverage kept up. On May 22, the New York *Times*, in an editorial headlined "Bankruptcy Is Not a Weapon," declared:

Can the bankruptcy law become a tool for breaking unions? That's what organized labor says will happen unless Congress amends the law to protect union contracts in what are called Chapter XI reorganizations. Some of labor's friends in Congress take this threat seriously. But it's likely that labor's immediate goal is to keep wages high in the ailing airline

industry, even if that means fewer jobs. Congress would be
wise to pause before rushing judgment . . .

Bankruptcy reorganizations are serious medicine. A
corporation's assets come under court control and management is subject to dismissal by the court. Creditors, including
unions, must be satisfied before the stockholders see a penny
— incentive enough, one expects, to insure that bankruptcy
petitions are not just gimmicks. The real dangers would come
if labor were given precedence over other creditors in a bankruptcy. Where labor is intent on defending industry-wide
wage patterns rather than jobs — as seems the case with airlines — such precedence would give national unions the
power to force vulnerable companies into liquidation. . . .

The labor movement hardly took this lying down. In a letter to
the *Times* the next day, Victor Gotbaum, executive director of District Council 37, AFSCME, delivered his own thunderbolt:

Labor does not seek amendments to gain preference over
other creditors. One change called for is to prevent corporations from tearing up union contracts simply by filing for
bankruptcy. The Supreme Court in the *Bildisco* decision ruled
management could do this with no responsibility to
restore wages and benefits slashed or eliminated if the
bankruptcy petition is denied several months later. Your
vision of 'powerful unions' forcing companies into liquidation
defies understanding. . . . It would be foolish to force a battle
over whether workers or creditors should have priority. The
battle in these times is to keep solvent corporations afloat for
creditors, workers, stockholders and society. The court ruling
you endorse deprives workers of collective bargaining rights
and places their working lives in the hands of entrepreneurs
for easy manipulation, less regulated than a stock or bond . . . .

As the debate grew, organized labor declared that relief from
the court decision was its top lobbying priority of the year. And
labor won a victory. A House-Senate conference committee, ap-
proving a major overhaul of the Federal bankruptcy system, recommended passage of a bill that would require employers to negotiate
with their unions before breaching contracts in a bankruptcy action.

The bill overturned the high court ruling which gave employers the right to void their labor contracts unilaterally when declaring bankruptcy. The bill required permission of a bankruptcy judge before contracts could be abrogated. The judge would then have to determine that the employer had tried to negotiate concessions from the workers, that the concessions were necessary to avoid financial collapse, and that the unions had refused "without good reason."

The unions lost out on some elements of the bill. For example, the new law does not apply to cases still before the courts. In other words, the compromise applied only to future cases. The bill also set deadlines for the courts to decide contract issues. In addition, the bill allowed companies to dissolve their contracts with the union if the judge missed the deadline.

But as an official of the National Association of Manufacturers warned, "The test is going to be what happens in bankruptcy courts."

I have stressed this matter because it has not only been precedent-setting in terms of management-labor relations but because it's a graphic illustration of the straits that unions may well be facing in the years ahead. Labor should not cause faltering companies to go bankrupt, nor do I think that it really wants to. But unless labor sees clearly that it is under the most intense pressure to adopt an attitude of cooperation and partnership with management, the future looks stormy indeed. If the Supreme Court can decide to restructure the traditional business-labor relationship by permitting bankruptcy cancellations of union contracts, little more argument is needed to point out labor's fragile line of defense in an adjusting economy.

Is Labor Getting the Gut Message?

While many corporations were expected to rack up major profits in 1985, they were still up against high labor costs which reduced their ability to compete with rivals both at home and abroad. Contracts for about 535 different companies covering some 2.4 million unionized workers were due for renewal. Management negotiators early in the year were insisting that making their companies competitive would be the key aim in contract negotiations. That meant, of course, some form of concessions and a reasonable lid on demands for wage increases.

It would not be easy.

There were also some special reasons why corporations could not yield to demands for wage increases and still remain competitive. Deregulation of basic industries had led to new non-union competition and this was pressuring negotiations not only in the affected industries but others as well. There was also that muscle-bound dollar of ours which had the undesirable effect of making imports less costly than our home products, severely affecting our trade balance.

The choice was clear, if treacherous. "Competition has forced employers who had a lot of market power to be much more careful about wage increases," predicted Aubrey Freedman, labor economist for the Conference Board, the nonprofit research group. The Conference Board, after sampling labor experts, reported that the outlook for wages and benefits for unionized workers was an increase on the average of about 4 percent in 1985, up somewhat from 1984's 3.6 percent. That would make the gain less than the 6.5 percent rise forecast for employees' salaries in 1985, and less than the year's expected inflation rate, predicted to be about 4.5 percent to 5 percent.

The year was not far along when an encouraging note was sounded by a report adopted at a meeting of the executive council of the AFL-CIO. Its thrust appeared to be an effort to reshape the labor movement for the post–industrial age.

More than two years in preparation, the report called on the unionized labor movement to explore alternatives to the traditional "adversarial collective bargaining relationship." This could lead to giving up comprehensive contracts in favor of minimum guarantees that will serve as a floor for individual bargaining. The aims were to give union members some leeway for independence and personal initiative and companies the opportunity and flexibility to better reward the most productive workers.

Among other provisions the report urged unions to identify and address such newer issues of worker concern as pay inequity or comparable worth and health and safety standards. Another recommendation sought programs on "quality of work life" to give employees some say in the job environment. A call was made for establishing new categories of union membership for workers not in organized bargaining situations. The aim here was to allow those who left unionized jobs to retain a union affiliation. Or it could permit workers who voted for the union in an unsuccessful representation election to have a union affiliation.

It was obvious, despite expressed pessimism among some of the labor officials who voted for the report, that the AFL-CIO executive council was eager to provoke some fresh thought. A sense of coming to terms with reality had clearly entered the council's deliberations, and it was high time.

But at the same meeting in late February, 1985, there was also expressed a rising demand for getting back what had been given away in concessions in prior years. Reports of economic growth and higher profits of American corporations were fueling labor's hopes that it was time for its members to get what was coming. A typical comment was that of William Wynne, president of the United Food and Commercial Workers, some of whose members had given up $2.40 an hour in wage concessions in the 1982 contract. "We want to start reclaiming what's ours," Wynne declared.

Other labor leaders fell in line, such as Owen Bieber, president of the United Auto Workers Union, who said, tersely enough, "Chrysler workers can't be deterred." The Chrysler workers' goal, as the seventy thousand employees looked at the company's record $2.4 billion profit in 1984, was to match gains made by employees at Ford Motor and General Motors in 1984.

Was labor looking through two different "scopes" at one time? Was labor taking both a long-range look at what might be needed for years to come while simultaneously pushing for short-term satisfaction as it demanded the return of concessions? It was hard to fault the Chrysler workers for wanting to obtain the gains they gave up. The gap between the two viewpoints was worrisome, especially in a "heavy bargaining" year.

Were both business and labor gearing to face each other again in their usual hard-nosed way? Wasn't there a "gut message," I couldn't help thinking, that was being ignored? That message seemed crystal clear, the need for rapport to give the country a chance to become a viable domestic and international producer.

Jerry J. Jasinowski, executive vice president and chief economist for the National Association of Manufacturers, laid out that "gut message" some months earlier in a sort of "Op-Ed" piece in the

Sunday business section of the New York *Times*:

> With the recent decline in unemployment, a return to profitability in major industries and the wage concessions of recent years, the temptation may be to think wage costs can take off again. The result would seriously exacerbate competitive problems and threaten the employment gains that have occurred during this recovery. Real job security will result only from being competitive. Furthermore, an escalation of wages would raise the inflation rate; and the increase in inflation would probably provoke a restrictive monetary policy response on the part of the Federal Reserve, prompting an economic slowdown.

It seemed to me that this message was a realistic one which should reach everyone on both sides of the negotiating table. Would anyone listen?

Labor Has No Other Choice

It isn't necessary to recap at this point all of the problems organized labor has had in the last decade and a half. The bald fact is that organized labor cannot survive unless it adopts new attitudes and behavior patterns that will create a working partnership with management. Unions can only lose if they continue their traditional adversarial policies. Business, however, can survive if labor doesn't go along. Yet many companies pursuing a hardening relationship with labor will undergo trauma after trauma in the process.

If the head-to-head confrontation persists, American society will be the ultimate victim. Unions will keep losing members and union jobs will continue to disappear. Companies will move into the nonunion area and displaced workers will increasingly become another disadvantaged segment of the country's population.

Intransigence on one side of the bargaining table inevitably causes intransigence on the other. The only way to avoid the destructive collision that follows is to consider the realities of the situation and react with some common sense.

So far, I am sorry to say, common sense has not been much in evidence.

Recently my firm represented a manufacturing company near Boston. The 125-employee firm had been negotiating with a Steelworkers' local for about six weeks toward the end of the contract's duration. The company told the union leadership that it couldn't afford any wage increases and supported its position by showing the union the company's books. The union, however, had adopted Lane Kirkland's motto of "no concessions" even before negotiations began. The leadership even spurred the rank and file to hope for some substantial increases.

Despite the company's difficult economic situation, the union's final negotiating demand was for a wage increase of $1 an hour in each of the three years of the contract. Management refused. A bitter seven-week strike ensued. During the strike the union tried to engage in illegal picketing, massing at the exits and entrances of the company's offices.

The company had a definite production schedule. It would simply have to close down if it did not get its orders out. In a last-ditch effort to stay alive, the company hired permanent replacements for those out on strike. It just did not have the assets to wait out the strike. Large companies in major industries such as steel, rubber, trucking, and automotive may have the resources to ride out a storm, but this manufacturer did not. The company replaced about 50 percent of the strikers. This action meant that many strikers couldn't get their jobs back even when the strike ended.

During the walkout we continued to negotiate and I told the union leaders that the way things stood we were between a rock and a hard place. This is the way I laid out the situation.

> If the company "won," it would permanently replace all of the strikers and continue to operate. The union would be on the outside looking in. The union would be likely to lose its representation rights because the new hires would probably not support the union.
>
> If the union *"won,"* the company would be out of business and the employees who struck would lose their jobs anyway. This could happen either of two ways:
>
> One — The company would be unable to accept the union's $1-an-hour wage demand because it would be unable to work, produce its wares, and distribute them at a profit.

The company would therefore have to close its doors. In that case, both the union and its members, as well as the employer, would be the losers.

Two — If the company agreed to the union's wage demand, it would soon find itself on a downhill slide into bankruptcy. The company's economic lifeline was very fragile and could not support the pull of a hefty wage increase.

Facing those unhappy scenarios, the union, after some weeks of consideration, called me to ask for another meeting. During the discussion that followed, the union leaders came to realize that the company wasn't going to capitulate and would go out of business rather than accede to impossible demands. The union called off the strike. Contract talks resumed and an agreement followed. The company got about 95 percent of what it wanted. It agreed to wage increases of $.20 an hour the first year, $.20 an hour the second year, and $.15 an hour the third year. These represented a total wage gain of 2.5 percent.

In addition, management successfully bargained for modification of work rules. In the new contract, management regained the right to have employees work overtime if necessary. Previously, the employees could refuse to work overtime and most of them did refuse. The change gave the company more flexibility and the opportunity to function with fewer people than was possible in the past. What does this particular case show?

At least 50 percent of the workers who went out on strike were angered because they lost their jobs to permanent replacements. With unemployment high at the time, there were plenty of aspirants eager to obtain employment. The other 50 percent who returned to work were upset because they had struck for seven weeks, lost wages, and the $.20-an-hour increase the first year would not even begin to make up the lost wages and benefits. The likelihood is that they will never be made up.

All of the workers were certainly resentful because they realized afterwards that their union leaders had led them down the wrong track. The union leaders fueled the resentment that resulted in a strike, in which both the union and the workers lost. Conversely, all the workers were angered at the employer because he had won and had, at least in part, been responsible for the strike which cost them so much inconvenience, pain, and lost wages.

Unfortunately, the union's tough stance created a no-win situation from the outset. Moreover, after a seven-week strike, it was very difficult to erase the "us against them" relationship. The lingering attitude from such strikes is almost always, "We'll get you next time." The bitter aftertaste doesn't bode well for peaceful relationships when the new three-year contract ends.

How different it would have been if the union leadership had taken seriously management's claim that it couldn't afford a $1-an-hour wage gain every year for three years. In retrospect, it would have helped everyone. Negotiations could have taken a different tack, resulting in a smaller wage gain but continued full employment. The employees would not have resented either their union leaders or the employer to the extent they did afterwards. The company could have continued to operate without interruption so that it could stay alive and compete.

Does organized labor have any other choice? Do company owners have any other choice but to do what they must to survive and remain viable, competitive entrepreneurs?

Quite candidly, it seems to me that the only way that unions can become working partners with management is to change their internal politics. Union leaders, as I said before, virtually have to promise pie in the sky, often in total disregard of the true economic picture, just to keep their elective positions. A working partnership of management and labor will not come into being as long as top union leaders insist on "no concessions" and talk of four-day workweeks and more paid holidays at a time when American industry is struggling to improve productivity to compete effectively in international markets.

Is a Partnership of Management and Labor Possible?

After nearly two decades in the management-labor negotiating process, I find myself reluctantly compelled to ask this question. Is a labor partnership with business possible? Frankly, I don't think so.

Unless —

Unless either the top labor chiefs and the mass of membership can clearly face reality and decide that only a new attitude encompassing mutual management-labor goals will save them and help restore the national economy to its rightful place in world markets.

Lane Kirkland and William Winpisinger may be truly interested in a partnership with management and might participate in a national policy conference or even a Presidential commission. Yet one might ask whether their harshly independent rhetoric has already so affected the rank-and-file workers that they will find it difficult to accept a new tone of moderation.

Another question comes to mind. Can the union heads become more moderate? It's hard to tell because labor is beginning to speak with two voices. In a September, 1984, article in *Parade* magazine, Douglas Fraser, the former president of the United Auto Workers Union, observed, "The future of the labor movement will be determined by its capacity to change with time and events." Indeed, that is the case.

Yet when asked to react to the serious challenges facing unionism, Kirkland told *Parade* "I have never felt any sense of doom and gloom. In the 1920s, unions were supposedly dying because we couldn't organize the semi-skilled workers on the assemblyline. Now, we're 'on the way out' because we can't organize more educated, more skilled workers. It's the same damned thing. You cannot organize until the changes are in place. We always catch up, and I can't think of any reason that won't be true in the future." *Do we always catch up?*

Fraser than added, "In the future, fewer solutions are going to be found at the bargaining table. We're going to find them in the political process. Negotiations cannot solve basic social problems like national health insurance, national unemployment programs or Social Security." *Will the political process help unions after large numbers of rank-and-filers rejected union recommendations and voted twice for Republican Presidential candidates?*

"Politics is not going to replace what the labor movement lacks," declared Robert Schrank, a former machinist and now a labor-management consultant. "The labor movement lacks vision. They have no idea who the new worker is, who is in a full-scale flight from blue-collar work." *Lack of vision or refusal to change?*

While the two voices speak in widely different terms, we must be encouraged by the light and clarity of some statements made by a few unionists. Ultimately, it is the individual worker's security and that of his or her family which is most threatened by the failure to reach out to a new rapport. Perhaps the rank and file of organized labor must be persuaded most of all of the need for management-labor rapport. I referred to this in an earlier chapter. The most promising sign that many workers understand the need for better relations with management is that the union membership voted its conscience rather than its leadership's in the last two Presidential elections. One may hope and pray that the changing mix of people in unionism, the younger element, the greater number of women and minorities, will look at their relationship with employers without going back to the old ways but with a more enlightened, independent viewpoint.

Personally, I am very hopeful that this will happen, as I am that the new voices in the labor movement will be heard more often. Perhaps it is within the realm of possibility that the old-timers, including the very top union brass, will wake up to the urgent needs in the management-labor arena before it's too late.

In the meantime, there's the tough matter of perception on the part of the public. Who's the bad guy on either side of the table? Are managers viscerally antiunion? Are unions intransigent to the point of no return? Are unions here to stay?

In that regard I want to conclude this chapter with some excerpts from a *Face the Nation* telecast over the Columbia Broadcasting System on December 4, 1983. Leslie Stahl hosted the program. The participants were John Naisbitt, author of *Megatrends*, the highly successful book on new directions in American society; Studs Terkel, the author of *Working*, a book on how Americans regard their jobs; and I.

STAHL: Do you think that there is a national management conspiracy to bust or break the unions?

TERKEL: There doesn't have to be a conspiracy. I wish it were as simple as that. No, the climate is set and the climate is set, of course, by the most outrageous anti-labor administration within memory. And so we have not apple blossom time, but certain union-busting time.

STAHL: Yes, but the public seems to be behind this, not just the administration.

TERKEL: That's precisely the point. I think there's been a lobotomy performed down through the years, as far as unions and labor are concerned, ever since World War II, and it's changed. Big business has become more sophisticated in the person of Mr. Cabot, say, in contrast to a guy Henry Ford hired in the thirties to fight UAW, Harry Bennett, who would hire thugs and ex-cons with baseball bats to bust the heads of picketeers. Today you have smiling, three-piece suit guys doing the same job, so much more sophisticated. The result, the young members of the work force have no idea how the minimum wage came to be. They think it came as an apple in the hand of Eve in the Garden of Eden.

It was bloody heads that did it and guys that were blacklisted, and so minimum wage came to be and that's under attack today. There's definitely a union-busting climate, no doubt in my mind.
STAHL: Mr. Cabot, did you hear what Studs Terkel just said about you? He compared you to the thugs of days gone by. Are you a union buster?
CABOT: No, I'm not, Leslie, and I think that it's about time in our society to look at the real issues. I don't believe I'm any more a union buster than perhaps Mr. Winpisinger and the other members of the AFL-CIO, because they struck Greyhound Lines, would like to be considered a company buster.
STAHL: But you do go into companies and you advise them how to keep unions out or how to get them out. Now you admit that.
CABOT: I think you're mischaracterizing what I do. I am an attorney that represents management to provide management their legal and practical and strategic options. In some cases, it is to represent companies who desire to maintain their nonunion status. In other words, it's to represent companies like Greyhould who wish to know their rights when the union strikes a particular company.
STAHL: But also you work to keep unions out.
CABOT: Yes, I do. If that is what the company's objective is, and the union seeks to organize
STAHL: You don't tell them to hire a lot of women and not to hire Blacks.
CABOT: I do not. What I do suggest is management pay attention, careful attention, to the hiring process to hire people who'll be compatible to the company's objectives, but in terms of specifically zeroing in and saying women, Blacks, old, young, that's ridiculous.
STAHL: John Naisbitt, you forecast the future, your crystal ball. What's going to happen to unions? Are they becoming obsolete?

NAISBITT: Well, I think the evidence suggests that we're moving toward an almost union-free society. This was not started by Ronald Reagan. This has been going on for a long time. You know the United States was never very unionized, certainly by European standards. I think it was 32 percent at the height of the industrial period.

Then it started to slide. It went down 20 percent a few years ago. Today, in the private sector, only 16 percent of the work force is unionized, and in the economically dynamic South and West, only about 7 or 8 percent is unionized. There are about 85 percent of the people in this country who are working and are not members of unions in the private sector.

STAHL: And it's moving fast in that direction.

NAISBITT: It's moving very fast in that direction and will continue to move there unless unions reconceptualize what their role is in the society, unless that changes.

STAHL: Studs, what would happen if we had no unions in the United States?

TERKEL: We would be very simply a fink society. Let's be honest about it. Let's call things by their proper names. "Union Free" is the wrong phrase, I advise Mr. Naisbitt. It would be scab enthralled, the way it was way back. How did unions come to be and why did they come to be? What chance does an individual workman or workwoman have against a conglomerate? Who's kidding who? Muhammed Ali in his prime in the same ring with a flyweight and let the best man win. That's why unions came to be in the first place.

NAISBITT: You're talking as if we used to all be unionized and we're talking about not being unionized. There are very few people in this country that are unionized today.

TERKEL: I agree.

NAISBITT: 84 percent. And 84 percent of the working force of this country are not finks.

TERKEL: I agree with you. That's the sad part of it. I think we have to go deeper, beyond Reagan, I agree. We're antihistorical. We have no sense of past. This applies to every aspect of our lives and certainly our labor past. We have no idea how people got whatever they have, union conditions or minimum wage, how it came to be. And once you have this no sense of past, born yesterday — not even yesterday; there is no yesterday — you're bound to have this.

CABOT: Studs, I'm surprised you don't give the workers of our country enough credit, the workers in the eighties, and don't confuse and talk about the thirties — we're in the 1980s and the workers today are brighter and more independent than ever before. And they're not going to take any baloney from management any more or less than they're going to be misled by baloney from labor unions, and if we take a look at that worker, management needs that worker in order to survive, in order for all of us to survive. And if we're going to expect to be competitive in our society, and have productive workers, then it's an absolute non sequitur to say that that worker is going to be abused by management. On the contrary, management is going to have to treat that worker better than before, with or without a labor union, in order to be competitive today.

TERKEL: I'd like to comment on Mr. Cabot. I'm delighted that you respect the intelligence of working people. I do too. But intelligence also concerns an awareness of history itself, and if people, no matter how intelligent they are, are deprived of certain aspects of our background and life, they're bound to be taken now and then.

By the way, I want to correct you, Leslie, I never referred to Mr. Cabot as a thug. On the contrary, he's charming and handsome, and wears a three-piece suit, and that's the big difference between the thirties and now; much more sophisticated big business has learned many things. Labor has lagged in that respect.

STAHL: Can somebody talk, though, about the possibility that without unions there will not be a middle class in this country. Mr. Naisbitt, do you see that as a problem?

NAISBITT: Well I think that's also holding it either/or. We're at the beginning of a new economy, a whole new period; we've been changing economies. This is not a recovery; this is the new economy overtaking the old, and much of the unions are in the old industrial economy, and that will continue to slide and that's one of the reasons union membership as a function of the work force will continue to go down.

We're in a period of working all this out, just as we were when we started the industrial revolution. A lot of farmers in this country came to the cities and we changed to an industrial economy and they took less pay and it was the unions that helped crank that pay up. I think there are going to be other instrumentalities this time around.

CABOT: There is a serious misconception that I'm hearing; that is the idea of polarization. Management making a lot, workers not. I think we have to look at the reality of the situation. The idea that workers or management should expect to give or take every year, and it's automatic, is absolutely ludicrousness. It's ridiculous. We have to look at what people get or don't get by whether or not the company is competitive and productive and able to afford to give whatever it can give. It cannot do what companies did in the sixties and seventies by giving, passing on to the consumer, mortgaging its present in the hope of borrowing to pay; that is destined to produce another recession, and probably even worse, unless we learn from our mistakes.

CHAPTER XI

PRODUCTIVITY, ROBOTICS, OR — ?

"You can imagine the consequences should we develop a robot unit with an IQ of 110."

The Specter Looms

Next to unemployment, the fear that most racks American workers is robotics.

Whether it's in the union meeting halls or during plant coffee breaks, at just plain bull sessions or in nightmares, the vision of a series of smoothly functioning robots deftly "manning" an assembly line or a complete plant, dismays workers, unionized or not. Workers see themselves looking on hopelessly from the outside as robots do the jobs they once did, and do them better.

I have found that this fear is often caused by lack of understanding on the part of the employer and/or the union. Sometimes an employer's reluctance to speak honestly about his automation plans causes his workers to fear robotics. Now and then an employer will even use the threat of robotics to exact greater productivity from his workers.

Automation became a key issue in negotiations between a hospital, which I represented, and its union employees. One of the union's demands was that if the hospital became computerized or adopted other forms of automation, the current employees should be given the first opportunity for retraining. The union was clearly trying to protect itself and provide for the security of its members. The employer, however, knew that if he granted that demand, he would be binding himself to a course of action that might backfire against him in an uncertain future.

Management took the position that it couldn't automatically grant its workers the opportunity for retraining because some of their skills and achievement levels might be insufficient for the new jobs and make the exercise a waste of time. The union almost went out on strike because management rejected the demand. After due investigation, the employer decided to give first consideration to the current employees but not to preclude himself from selecting others from the outside. The union raised hell, but finally complied after it came to understand the employer's dilemma.

In another automation case the employer was at fault. My client was a lamp manufacturer in the process of computerizing his office. The likelihood was that some employees would lose their jobs. Yet he refrained from telling them about this possibility because he feared an angry confrontation. When word finally leaked out, all the office workers jumped to the conclusion that once computers were installed, most of them would be out pounding the pavement in search of new jobs. Tempers flared and battlelines seemed about to be drawn.

Facing the situation head on, the employer decided to tell the employees that only a mere handful would be affected and the majority would continue as before. The confrontation faded away and peace was restored. It was only the initial lack of frank communications that threw a monkey wrench into otherwise friendly labor relations.

In a third case a productivity consultant had an effect just about diametrically opposed to the one intended. He was hired to train workers at a plant in New Jersey so that they would become more productive. He appeared one day, dressed in a natty, blue, three-piece, pinstripe suit, with white shirt and fancy tie. When he spoke to the employees, he looked as if he had just left his Madison Avenue office. This sophisticated, articulate man, with elegant gray hair, would have fit right in with the advertising crowd. But he was a

fish out of water trying to talk to the generally unskilled, unedu-
cated workers of this plant.

His listeners were soon turned off and showed their dis-
pleasure. Nasty, even bitter remarks were directed at him from the
floor. It was obvious that the workers were quickly convinced that
the consultant was in a different world and had no idea of their
problems on the production line.

That particular incident taught me some important lessons. It
taught me that the change in attitudes toward new technologies
that increase productivity is going to come slowly in many quarters.
In the New Jersey plant, management couldn't reasonably expect
to hire a high-powered consultant to come into a plant, wave a
magic wand, and suddenly solve the productivity problem. It also
showed me that poor management can poison the attitude which
workers bring to their jobs. This circumstance alone can cause a
drop in productivity.

I am convinced that if employees can see that increased
mechanization is really needed for the company to compete either
in the domestic or international marketplace, the tension so often
aroused by automation will diminish. Once employees see the
need for automation, they will begin to understand that they have
no other choice if they expect to keep jobs within a plant or office.
Productivity training must begin with management, who, in turn,
must carry the message to the workers and from then on involve
them as much as possible in the overall effort.

This brings me to the much-feared specter of robotics. In an
effort to improve productivity, recourse to automation to replace
people represents a failure on both sides to achieve competitiveness. A failure? Yes, because low productivity invariably results
from one or more of the following three factors: lack of dynamic
management; labor costs and conditions that have an adverse
impact on productivity and competitiveness; and eroding worker
motivation.

Would increased productivity mitigate against the need for
robotics? Very likely it would, although I recognize that there are
cost and efficiency factors to robotics that cannot be ignored. But
the use of electronic and mechanical automation is very expensive,
too. On a recent visit to a small Midwest plant where a dozen
assembly line workers had been employed, I noticed that the mini-

robotics process had trimmed the staff to only two or three. They were pushing the buttons which operated the robotic arms lifting heavy parts and even assembling parts. I asked the plant manager how it was working. "Fine, so far, but it's expensive," he replied. "Will it pay off?" I asked. He shrugged. "Over a period of time; if we can push our output enough, we ought to be able to recoup the cost," he said.

While that plant had pretty well gone to so-called "steel-collar workers," my own assessment up to this point is that robotics has made only a minor presence on the American work scene. There were problems with it, too, besides the cost, stemming from application and adaptation. Workers perceive robotics much more fearfully than they should. This is particularly the case when efforts to hike productivity could be a powerful inducement to avoid robotics.

What Is Robotics?

A robot operates with motorized, sensory, and elective or decision-making functions. But of all the robots now in use, between 30 to 35 percent only can be considered actual robots capable of performing more than basic, repeated, or programmed moves. Under almost all robotization programs, the devices are attached to fixed bases. Their weight and size requires that they remain attached to an immobile foundation.

Producers of robotics are now working to free their "creatures" from their moorings. Moving freely along an assembly line or plant area, mobile robots could eventually become a much more potent factor in productivity and flexibility and have a correspondingly greater effect on employment of human workers. That, however, may be some years, even a decade or so, off.

The growth rate in robotics usage varies sharply among forecasters. Some see a 35 percent growth between 1983 and 1988, or 10 percent less than 1984 estimates. Others project a 74 percent compound annual growth. This big gap in forecasts tends to underscore the volatility and speculation which surrounds the field of robotics. Venture capitalists, always eager to latch on to the newest technological innovations, are willing to supply the funds to robotics makers. However, the initial lack of profits among producers has tended to turn off many investors. But this isn't unusual in a burgeoning high-tech industry where developmental costs put a heavy hand on profits.

No doubt, the field holds out a glamourous market prospect which will increasingly attract a flow of funds, feeding research and development programs which, in turn, will lead to breakthroughs into more sophisticated systems.

In the meantime, the Japanese robot-making industry is undeniably better equipped than American and other manufacturers. Fired by the size and needs of their own domestic market and the potential abroad, the Japanese have already shown expertise in application, engineering, and cost strategy. Estimates are that by the end of 1985, Japan will have working more than 100,000 robots against about 15,000 in the U.S.

The Japanese application appears to be more problem-oriented and pragmatic than the American version. As Paul H. Aron, executive vice president of Daiwa Securities America, Inc., New York, told *Industry Week*: "Unlike their American competitors, the Japanese developed robots to solve particular production problems while American robots were solutions looking for problems that didn't find much application beyond material handling and automotive spot welding."

In addition, the Japanese industry has an added advantage in its more aggressive and ambitious attitude toward robots, according to Aron. For example, in 1982, the largest U.S. order for robots was 100 units from Chrysler Corporation. Toyota in Japan placed an order for 720 units. And while General Motors plans to have 14,000 units installed by 1990, Aron told *Industry Week*, Matsushita Electric Industrial Company is said to plan an installation of 100,-000 units by 1990.

In some added comments about the different timetables for installing robots between the two countries, Aron observed, "It's not a question of superior technology or resolve but rather one of cooperation between management and labor.

"A very large part of Japanese management has served in labor unions and many chief executives are former presidents of their company's union. Management understands that unions are a source of recruitment for supervisory personnel, which is not the case in America. Therefore, there is a greater recognition [by management] of labor's problems in Japan." Aron contends that

U.S. management has not yet assumed "the vital responsibility of retraining for robotics."

Are robots smarter than humans?

Compared to humans, robots have an IQ of about 70 whereas the IQ of most blue-collar workers ranges between 90 and 120. "About 10 percent (of blue-collar employees) have an IQ of 90 and another 10 percent stop somewhere short of 110," observes Toshio Kohno, president of Dainichi Machinery Company, a leading Japanese robot producer, when quoted in *Newsday*, the Long Island, New York, newspaper.

In Kohno's view, a human with a 70 IQ can perform simple, repetitive tasks, but if an object such as a rock gets in the way, he or she won't pick it up unless told to do so. An IQ of 80 to 90 is required for the decision to take away the obstacle without being ordered to. But "if a sensor device and discrimination function were built into the basic robot," Kohno said, "it would be able to make such decisions as well as people do."

He added, "With present sensor technology, it is possible to produce robots with an IQ of close to 90. But you can imagine the consequences should we develop a robot unit with an IQ of 110."

That day may be only a year or two away, he believes, although, even with an IQ of 100, machines which are highly specialized can perform sophisticated tasks. A special feature of robots is their memory. They can, for example, be programmed to store away experiences of the past for instant recall, allowing them to adjust quickly to new, apparently unexpected situations.

The Japanese expert cautioned that all this didn't mean that robots were poised to replace flesh-and-blood workers. Immobile as most are, the robots will occupy a large area of factory floor. He estimated that for twenty different operations, twenty types of robots would be required, occupying large areas of expensive floor space in factories. In Japan, he pointed out, the high price of land remains the single greatest obstacle to the widespread use of robotics.

Presumably, in the U.S. the cost of land would not be as much of a problem since many automotive plants and other heavy industries are in outlying areas where land is relatively cheap.

But as far as Japan and Toshio Kohno are concerned, the answer lies either in free-moving robots capable of various functions and in the development of "new, lightweight materials to remedy this situation," he said. "Presumably, with lighter materials, we can develop more compact models but there's still no easy solution in sight. Modern robotics is still very much in the stone age."

In the U.S. profits have eluded robotics producers because of the high cost of customizing each robot to perform its particular task, often twice the price of the robot itself. Partly because of this cost problem, the U.S. is third in the world of robotics use, not only far behind Japan but also the Soviet Union. Unlike the governments of those two countries, governments intimately involved in industry and pushing production, our government has typically expressed a hands-off policy.

The Defense Department has publicly stated that while it recognizes that the U.S. is running well behind in the development and use of robotics, the government's role should be "supportive and nurturing rather than directive and regulatory." It said that it views robotics not as an isolated technology but as an integration of a wide range of technologies and disciplines, including computer hardware and software, servos, actuators, and sensors.

Yet the House Science and Technology Committee's subcommittee on investigations and oversight predicted that the extensive use of robots will have major impacts on productivity and could create jobs. "But it also has a great potential to displace workers. The extent of such displacements is not clear, but what is clear is that robots will dramatically alter employment patterns in at least some basic industries, such as autos," the subcommittee said.

Dr. Edith Martin, Deputy Undersecretary of Defense for Research and Advanced Technology, said that she was not certain that a national plan would facilitate meaningful advances in robotics technology. She told Congress during a hearing that the Defense Department believes that the government should rely on the incentives of the free enterprise system to encourage the use of robots where there is an economically sound reason for it. "Robots shouldn't be installed simply because someone considers it fashionable to do so."

Toshio Kohno went much further in speculating how humans and robots will coexist in the work place.

When he was asked by Keiji Ikehata, a staff writer for the

Japanese magazine *Ekonomisuto,* if robot producers had a responsibility to society in view of the potentially destructive impact of robotics, Kohno replied frankly. "We are producing cold machinery but our factories are run by human beings. Production must be geared to the welfare of an interdependent human community, whether a super-robot is developed or not. The secret is learning to live together in organic harmony. If we makers refuse to do this, then our factories are doomed to become vast inorganic machines where human beings have no place. Sure enough, our workers will be replaced by robots.

"If we are really committed to the idea of humanity, then we must strive to create a more human work environment. In the end, there is a fundamental difference between men and machines. Robots don't have the same psychological or emotional attributes. They aren't capable of the subtle nuances of human thought and feeling.

"Good entrepreneurship requires first and foremost an abiding commitment to the worker as a member of the human community. If automation is pursued relentlessly in the name of profits alone, factory workers may find themselves transformed into automatons. But when this happens, the true leaders of industry will step into the breach and restore the balance. After all," he concluded, "we're not stupid."

But Then Again . . .

So much for robotics, the science and practice of robots, and its evolution. But while some like Toshio Kohno feel robot use is still in the stone age, others take a much more positive view of its progress. "The human race is now poised on the brink of a new industrial revolution in its impact on mankind," declared James Albus, head of the robotics research laboratory at the National Bureau of Standards. If one takes such a sweeping statement literally, it's not hard to believe that robotics could have a very deep, widespread effect on the American work scene. And if that's the case, the effect could be profound on collective bargaining and labor legislation.

Robots have a definite place and function in certain types of plants, assuming duties that are onerous and boring to human workers. They can produce more because they can perform at a faster pace than their flesh-and-blood counterparts and do not grow weary. They aid safety, too, by taking over hazardous jobs. They can increase quality by eliminating human error. In addition, while the cost of adaptation is high, they are cost-effective in a growing number of cases.

Robot makers insist that economy is the primary reason to install robots. Joseph F. Engelberger, of Unimation, Inc., of Danbury, Connecticut, told *INC. Magazine* in 1982, "Conventional machines, if they exist to perform a particular job, may cost three to five times as much as a robot. One aerospace firm, for example, is using an $85,000 robot for work that would otherwise require a $300,000 machine. And once installed, conventional machines resist change. In the past automobile manufacturers had to shut down for months in order to retool assembly lines. Now because robots are easily reprogrammed, the same result can sometimes be achieved in days. . . .

"If you buy a $50,000 robot," he continued, "pay for the loan, install the robot, depreciate it, maintain it, overhaul it and give it an eight-year life, the total cost is $6 an hour. The ordinary automobile worker, by contrast," he said, "now costs an employer about $19 an hour. General Motors says that it's going to have 14,000 robots by 1990," he said. "If they could do it just one year sooner, it would earn $728 million per year in savings."

Whether one accepts either the "stone age" or the "profound impact" view of the current state of robotics, there are obviously concerns about the displacement of workers, the effect on collective bargaining, and what would happen to employees who lose their jobs. The only difference between the two views is simply the matter of time or how long it will take to feel the effect.

I am worried that employers and employees could easily fall into the trap of inevitability. That is, they could accept the growing presence of robotics as unstoppable, necessary, and perhaps generally helpful. It's the reverse side of the fear that many workers have about robotics, the sense that it just might be impossible to stop and the only thing to do is to hope that some redress for the human dislocation will be forthcoming.

Personally, I feel that this is not only foolish but also defeatist.

The important priority should be improving productivity and our competitive ability. Robotics certainly has a place in our industrial competitive ability. But its role will depend greatly on how much and how well American businessmen can improve their productivity through people. Currently the need for robotics seems large and widespread because of the country's fading international competitiveness. As the expertise of robot makers grows, there will be an inevitable rise in the number of devices used and in the number of applications in many fields. But a cap can be put on robotics, not only in mathematical terms but also in terms of efficiency, flexibility, and mental capability.

The solution, of course, depends on both producers and the unions, and how they handle a recognizable problem: fading productivity. Together and individually, they have not been creative enough in coping with that mutual problem. For an increasing number of producers, robotics looms as the panacea. But it isn't a cure-all.

I know a producer in the East who was having problems with his union and his competition. He decided that moving to the South into a completely automated plant would give him the cost and competitive edge he needed. But after detailed study, he concluded that there weren't enough skilled workers who could handle the intricate machines that would be used in the plant. A timetable showed that many months would be needed for start-up and his projected budget was so high that he realized he would be biting off more than he could chew. He stayed where he was, opting to cope with "the devils that he knew against the devils he didn't know."

Why won't robotics be for everyone?

First, the applications so far, and apparently for the near future, are geared to heavy industry, from steel-making to automobiles, from high-tech to middle-tech. Only major companies with very sizable assets will be equipped to fund such installations and to wait out the long period, as much as five years, for the payoff. This leaves the majority of American industry, where companies range in annual revenues from $5 million to $100 million, out of the picture. These companies will find it expensive and onerous to retool to the extent that they are producing largely by robotics.

Second, automation will necessarily be limited to relatively few applications in the service field, the largest growing segment of the American economy. Health care, travel, finance and insurance, retailing and merchandising in all its forms, leisure-time services, and other similar industries will continue to depend on human performance, with automation limited to the communications function in the form of computers, videos, and telemarketing. No "computers that do physical work," as one expert called robots, "will be able to perform the personal function that is the core basis for a service industry."

Third, robotics will need human operators not merely to push the buttons but to maintain and service the devices as well. The time to train, the length of the learning curve, and the cost of training will all be important factors to be fed into the economics of robotics installation. Other delaying factors include the ability to plan and develop the infrastructure to accommodate a galloping technology and the need to control it for anticipated productivity gains. This will mean some sweeping and time-consuming changes especially in the middle levels of management.

Will attrition and the alteration in jobs caused by the widespread shift to nonmanufacturing fields tend to offset the inroads of robotics? These are definite possibilities. On the other hand, if one were to sit around and wait to find whether that proposition was true, a good deal of valuable time could be lost in attacking the basic problem of productivity erosion.

Facing Up to the Challenge

If robotics is the unionized worker's greatest fear after unemployment, it is reasonable to assume that the threat of "steel-collar workers" will force American unions and their members to fight harder for job security than ever before. The inevitable result will be a toughening of the old adversarial relationship unless there are some intelligent efforts to bring both sides together.

I am urging my clients to form management-employee committees to address the issue of productivity and how it can be improved. This can be accomplished not only through formal committees but also through the device of quality circles.

I urge management to involve employees as much as possible in the discussion process for two key reasons. The first is that as longtime opponents meet to consider a mutual problem, it's likely that the basis for the problem, the emotional gut factors, will be laid out in the open and examined under a cold light. The emotion will give way to analysis and that will be the first step toward a solution. The second reason is that employees have always felt themselves outside the decision-making process and hence have reacted negatively to rules created unilaterally by management. Any effort to bring them into a dialogue will yield positive results.

Consider going even a step further by helping to form a management-labor institute, with offices and training facilities at various places in the U.S. A management-labor institute would provide a means for nonpolitical, nonthreatening, nonadversarial discussion. At first blush this may seem idealistic, a far out proposal to apply some basic, pragmatic thinking to a problem that appears too vast to solve.

The fact is that the issue of productivity vs. robotics, which can also be stated as the competitiveness of American productivity vs. the rest of the world's, won't be solved without drastic new approaches. A joint attack must be launched both by the producers, who are aware in their heads and hearts that robotics can only be adapted so far, and by unions eager not to be left out in the cold. Unions will have to take action or robotics will join the other forces which have put workers on the unemployment lines, cut union rolls, and created internal union tensions. Both management and labor should take the lead in educating workers about the need for greater productivity and the growing use of robotics. They must explain how robotics fits within the system now and can fit, without a vast job disruption, in the future. It is an absolute reality that the real burden of the problem must be shared by both management and labor. It's simply too expensive and too impractical for either to attack the problem alone.

The joint offensive won't be easy, primarily because of long built-in prejudices on both sides. Quality circles, including union representatives as well as employees and management, to explore production and quality control problems have proven very useful. This is particularly the case when they have been in existence and functioning before the start of contract talks. The bargaining table is simply not the best place to consider sensitive issues such as productivity.

Some people in management scoff at quality circles because they might tend to eliminate company pecking orders. Union heads are skeptical of quality circles because they might become just another union-busting technique. Such prejudices are old hat, haven't worked in the past, and will only worsen the problems that both sides face in the future. Simply stated, quality circles have the potential to bring both sides together.

An example of a new technique that is already helping to improve productivity is the so-called "Just in Time" method of inventory control. Adapted from the Japanese *kanban* system, the "Just in Time" method used in a growing number of American smokestack plants has reduced space requirements, labor, and overhead costs while maintaining or improving production. "Just in Time" eliminates the stocks of finished goods and production parts in stockrooms, warehouses, and other storage places. The process includes re-education of both plant management and workers. The emphasis on exercising better inventory control often focused directly on how much worker supervision was needed. Work teams operating under "Just in Time" required less supervision. In other words, the method gives workers more responsibility, not less, and makes them more responsive as they work more efficiently.

It's a good example of a new device to boost productivity and cut costs. Do we need to always go to Japan for such techniques or can we develop our own?

I believe we can develop our own.

CHAPTER XII

CLEARING THE AIR WITH NEW SEMANTICS

A Short Course in Human Relations

The Six Most Important Words:
"I Admit I Made a Mistake."

The Five Most Important Words:
"You Did a Good Job."

The Four Most Important Words:
"What Is Your Opinion."

The Three Most Important Words:
"If You Please."

The Two Most Important Words:
"Thank You."

The One Most Important Word:
"We."

The Least Important Word:
"I."

It should be self-evident that tempered, reasonable communications are the best means for building a bridge of understanding between opponents. Unless both parties to a dispute come to understand each other, there cannot be a productive resolution to the dispute. Ill-tempered, unreasonable expression has the opposite effect. If you were to listen to the typical exchanges between management and labor today, you would conclude that the contestants would be more at home in the Stone Age, communicating with grunts and clubs. When management and labor sit down to confer, the snarling contentiousness begins at once and rarely subsides. Each side seems irrevocably programmed into a nasty mode.

Let's take two traditional steps in the process, negotiating discussions and the grievance procedure.

In negotiations, the union "demands" and management "rejects." The union presents its laundry list and management immediately goes on the defensive. In recent years, management has taken the offensive, insisting on concessions which the union characteristically "rejects," at least initally. This demand-rejection syndrome is a game both sides have designed over the decades to keep the other off balance. It fosters competition, hostility, conflict, and hardening of the "us against them" attitude.

Wouldn't it be more productive if the process started with the union "requesting" management to consider possible changes to the existing, collective bargaining agreement? This would set a different tone to the talks, permitting management and the union to approach the discussions as a team. As a team, they could aim at productive resolutions rather than "victory" over each other. Would that the sage who said "a soft word turneth away wrath" had been a management-labor expert.

"Demand" has an edge to it so that management flatly says "no" or counters with its own demands to set the union back on its heels. That sets the negotiating exercise off to a bad start. When management rejects demands, resentment smokes in the eyes of union bargaining committees. This has happened many times. At the same time, if management summarily rejects a demand without a fair counteroffer, the union typically takes the position that the company isn't sincere and isn't bargaining in good faith. It's like an equation that leads nowhere: tough demands plus reluctant counteroffer equals zilch.

This unfortunate game has too often resulted in impasse and

strikes. In some situations workers wind up losing their jobs. In others employers are paying more than they can afford and are having irreparable harm done to their business. Unfortunately, the typical negotiation scenario has a built-in tendency toward confrontation because employees always anticipate that they will automatically get more in the new contract than they had in the old. Employers, on the contrary, want to give less and lately even take back some of the benefits of the earlier contract. Somehow, this squeeze play must be eased and preferably removed.

The typical grievance proceeding is no more conducive to cooperation than are contract negotiations. The very word "grievance" sets management's hair on end. Union negotiators may well have some honest grievances, but so do employers. If we drop the term grievance procedure for "problem-resolution," we begin to chart a course of cooperation. "Problem-resolution" connotes correction or rehabilitation or adjustment as opposed to an effort to discipline the other side. The "let's talk" approach is certainly conducive to solving problems that give rise to grievances (avoid the word if possible). Saying "there are some glaring inequities that must be changed," or words of that kind, is strictly confrontational and leads to the formation of battlelines. Nonadversarial, cooperative management-labor relations aim at finding mutually satisfactory solutions to problems. If an employee can intelligently and in a spirit of cooperation show management that something is wrong, it's likely a mutual attempt to correct the matter will find a just solution.

Both sides must agree that correction of an inequity or rehabilitation of a once better situation is preferable to punishing the other side. Management will have to sincerely want to negotiate sensitive matters. The union will have to realize that management is willing to meet it halfway.

The New Semantics

Isn't it funny, when the other fellow takes a long time to do something, he's slow. When I take a long time to do something, I'm thorough. When the other fellow doesn't do it, he's lazy. When I don't do it, I'm busy. When the other fellow does it without being told, he's overstepping his bound. When I go ahead and do it without being told, I'm showing

—177—

initiative. When the other fellow states his opinion strongly, he's bullheaded. When I state my opinion strongly, I'm firm. When the other fellow overlooks a few rules of etiquette, he's rude. When I skip a few rules of etiquette, I'm doing my own thing.

A New Management-Labor Lexicon

OLD	NEW
Demand	Request
Compete	Cooperate
Confront	Meet
Hostile	Problematic
Conflict	Resolve
Grievance	Problem-Resolution
Confrontation	Negotiation, Discussion
We/They, Us/Them	Team, All of Us
Employee	Associate
Worker	Staff Member
Open Door Policy	No-Door Policy
Foreman	Facilitator
I	We
Robot	Human Aid
Plant Discipline	Work Rules
Punitive	Rehabilitative
Top Down	Participative
Uniforms	Work Apparel
Middle Management	Planners, Expeditors
Department Meetings	Feedback or Speak–Up Meetings
Assume	Let's Discuss
Violation	Misunderstanding
Problem	Interruption
Reject	Needs Discussion
Refuse	Let's Talk

Expect	Needs Discussion
Isolation	Needs More Involvement
Work Reform	More Productive Ability
Improving Standards	Let's Be the Best
Work Ethic	Job Satisfaction
Lagging Productivity	We Can Be Better Doers
Tying Pay to Productivity	More Recognition for Good Work
Corporate Esprit	High Commitment
People Problems	Helping People Fulfull Themselves
Difficult Negotiations	Measuring Long-Term Implications of Short-Term Decisions
Subordinate	Team Members
Employee Handbook	Guidebook
Rules	Guidelines
Discipline	Counsel
Disciplining Report	Employee Contact Sheet
Time Clock	Recordkeeper
Firing	Separation
Training	Education, Development
Probation	Orientation
Seniority	Length of Service
Suspension	Remedial Action
Orders	Information Sharing
Directives	Goals
Personnel	Human Resources
Worker	Stakeholder
Job Description	Performance Guidelines
Evaluation	Job Appraisal

Note: All these terms are, of course, subject to individual adaptation in specific cases. Not all new versions will fit every situation. But as is obvious, the effort should be to turn the sharp edge of the traditional management-labor vocabulary to show a more positive surface so that the effect is inviting rather than deterring. Understanding, sensitivity, and a mixture of sympathy and empathy are at the heart of the matter. "Why don't we?" is certainly more constructive than "We've got to." "Let's" is better than "We must." "It seems" is better than "We find."

Word weaseling?

Maybe. I prefer to call it "word friendly." After all, what should we be seeking? "Confrontation" or (see the glossary) "Negotiation, Discussion." Got any better words? Let me encourage you.

The goal of nonadversarial labor relations is clear. Let me cite some excerpts from a March 1985 report by the President's Commission on Industrial Competitiveness:

> A skilled, motivated and secure work force is a prerequisite to realizing the dual goals of productivity and quality so crucial to maintaining the competitive advantage. . . . But more than a skilled and motivated work force, intelligent management, highly trained technical people, and *nonadversarial relations between labor and management are needed if U.S. industry is to be competitive.*

The italics are mine but the Commission study also said that competitiveness is determined in part by how effectively a nation's resources are used relative to its competitor's resources. According to the *Bureau of National Affairs Employee Relations Weekly*, the Commission found that "technological innovation, capital investment, and a fair trading environment help determine competitiveness, but *it is the people of the country — their knowledge, skill and will to excel — that determine how effectively that technology, capital and trade will be used.*" The italics again are mine.

Communications: Not a One-Way But a Two-Way Process

It's fine, of course, to use more positive semantics to inspire cooperation. The speakers also have to be sure that the others are listening, not resenting and reacting negatively to what is being said. Manner, tone, gesture, shouldn't contradict the new constructive vocabulary but should support it. Substance is vital, but so is the style in which it's delivered.

Too often I have sat in meetings and heard one side or the other "talking down" to the other. Nothing is more irksome than being patronized, because it denotes a lack of sincerity and real consideration. Some other caveats: Any new semantics would take on different features in different parts of the country. You may have to say things one way in the North, another way in the East or Midwest. Communications that are conducive to agreement have to take into consideration local mores. It's also important that the new terminology not seem legal or technical.

It's vital that the new semantics be simple and uncomplicated. It cannot have subtle, different, dual, or diverse meanings if it is to achieve harmony. And it's also very important that when the new words are used both sides recognize that neither can "assume" any hidden meanings nor take the content nor the speaker for granted.

Using the new semantics cannot be a one-shot affair. It won't work if it isn't repeated, reinforced, and continually followed up so that the message is understood and believed.

You may well ask whether words are everything. No, of course not. Actions still speak louder than words. But when a more positive set of words, terms, and expressions are used in negotiations, grievance procedures, and in every part of the working relationship between management and employees, some surprising, wholesome things can happen.

Skeptical? That's the wrong word. "Skeptical" gets you nowhere. Try "curious," "interested," or "open-minded." Any one of these is likely to get you started.

CHAPTER XIII

A HOW-TO-DO-IT FOR THE NONUNION COMPANY

"The strategy we designed emphasized a pro-company image, philosophy, and direction."

The smokestacker, the high-tech, or the low-tech company nestling away beyond the pale of organized labor has reason to feel confident that its labor problems are over. The percentage of workers belonging to unions has been declining for years. Unions themselves suffer from serious image problems. The public sees them as just another special interest group. For example, in 1984 the public strongly rejected a presidential candidate backed by most of organized labor ˙

But overconfidence can give birth to disaster. In fact, unionism could invade many companies which, one way or another, have avoided it. The straining arm of labor organization, flailing out desperately, has missed these companies and they think that the danger is past. It isn't.

Studies in the 1980s show that, despite the fact that many companies now feel that they are immune to unions, nonunion workers have a stronger perception than union members that unions are influential in running the United States and that unions are stronger than employers. Conversely, according to the *Journal of Labor Research*, union members have stronger perceptions that unions offer protection, job security, and improved wages and work conditions. Union members, more so than nonunion workers, have confidence in union leaders and believe membership is worth the cost in dues.

In addition, the *Journal* noted, nonwhite and blue-collar workers are more likely to join unions than whites and white-collar workers and are more likely to hold favorable views about unions and their leadership. But lack of familiarity with unions and the consequent reliance on stereotypes in forming their attitudes may lead nonunion workers to their generally unfavorable evaluation of unions, union activity, and union leaders, the *Journal* noted.

These attitudes may suggest a standoff between union and nonunion workers, but I don't think so. There are enough converging elements, such as the nonunion workers' perception of the political clout of unions and their paradoxical lack of familiarity with unions, to indicate that unionism poses a real hazard for the nonunionized company. When union organizers start knocking at the doors of the plant, pressing handbills on workers, and bringing to bear all their experience and pressure, nonunion employees may focus solely on their perception of the union as a source of strength and influence.

What's the answer to this possibility?

As I observed in Chapter VI on "The Nonunion World," organized labor is only the tip of the iceberg. As the tip goes, so does the iceberg. Whatever unions achieve in the world of organized labor inevitably invades the nonunion ranks. Accordingly, owners of nonunion companies have sought to keep pace with unionized companies in wages, benefits, and fringes. In many cases they have even exceeded union levels. At the same time, many nonunion companies have suffered because they have not given their employees a voice. Workers want management to listen to them. They want a greater form of representation than they have enjoyed. This is especially so because they have felt the clout of unionism.

To keep workers pro-company, management needs a plan of action, an offensive strategy. Even more important than whether a plant stays unorganized or goes union is the need to translate the aspirations of workers into motivation and productivity. No pro-company approach can succeed indefinitely without recognizing that nonunionized workers are as aware as union members of social change, improvements in life-style, and the rights of individuals. Ignoring the wants and needs of workers will not only open the doors to union organizers but also, and more urgently, eat away at productivity and competitive ability.

The following pages represent my experience and that of my colleagues in fostering a work climate among many companies which has served them and their workers well. Our goal has always been to create an environment that encourages employees to be pro-company, to identify his or her interests with those of the company, and to favor productivity and profitability.

Action Plan for a Human Resources Strategy

The strategy which we designed for the Midwest division of a manufacturing company emphasized a pro-company image, philosophy, and direction. The strategy took into account the company's rapid growth rate, its mixture of facilities, and significant variations in the management styles of the local facilities. Despite all these variables, the strategy succeeded in redirecting and refocusing the Midwest division's employee relations climate to a more positive pro-company environment. We involved the company's entire human resources staff in all phases of the plan so that its members would be fully trained to monitor the program's individual components in the future and implement the program in newly acquired or expanded facilities.

The components of the plan were:

Employee Relations Philosophy — The program is initiated with a statement to all employees over the signature of the division president. The statement endorses a philosophy which focuses on positive images of the organization and calls for the commitment to a loyal, dedicated work force. This statement, included in all handbooks and statements regarding benefits and personnel policy, formed the cornerstone of the human resources program.

Human Resources Audit System — This system develops

"climate" barometers by means of interviews with representative samples of local management. The interviews determine the existing employee relations environment and the needs for its redirection. Audits of all the facilities, union and nonunion, were expected to provide the desired sample.

Employee Benefits Kit — Concise descriptions of all fringe benefits are accompanied by step-by-step explanations of how employees obtain the benefits.

Revised Employee Handbook — The existing handbook was revised to reflect a more positive pro-company image. Special emphasis was put on explaining the value of becoming and remaining a company employee.

Human Resources Training — A training program was developed to address the division's communications needs and to improve the skills of first-level supervisors and administrators. The audits of local management regarding the employee relations environment revealed that supervisors needed training in a number of human resource areas. There were nine such areas: understanding workers; conducting informational, staff, and employee meetings; assertive communications; listening, exploring, and reflecting; eliciting day-to-day feedback from employees; conducting effective performance reviews; discipline; conflict resolution; and training in the efficient use of the company's employee profile and system for recruiting, screening and hiring.

Employee Profile — A cross section of managerial and supervisory personnel was interviewed in various locations to determine desirable and undesirable work-related attributes for company employees. This data was incorporated into the recruiting, screening, and hiring systems to serve as a basis for performance evaluation and advancement identification. The profile was then "prevalidated" through a survey of supervisory and managerial people to confirm that it contained pro-company attributes and desirable work performance characteristics of employees. The profile could be tailored to specific job classifications. After its validation and implementation, the profile was used to periodically track employees hired under its components.

Recruiting, Screening, and Hiring System — The validated and implemented employee profile formed the foundation of this system which revolved around positive reflections of the company's image and culture. The system was structured to ensure consistency in recruiting , screening, and hiring loyal and productive workers. The recruiting system called for the training of interviewers. We designed specific questions and taught interviewers to screen prospective employees to find out if they had the desired work-related attributes . Like the profile, the system was to be validated and monitored periodically to ensure its continuing effectiveness.

Employee Orientation System — The formal orientation program for new employees emphasized the company's management style, employee relations philosophy, and long-term organizational objectives. The supervisory audits revealed that orientation should go beyond a simple "get acquainted" period when employees would otherwise be preoccupied with learning routine job duties and responsibilities. The orientation program was expanded into an opportunity for employees to become thoroughly indoctrinated into the company's culture.

Checks and Balances — Setting up monitoring and follow-up procedures was recommended in order to evaluate the effectiveness of individual components and to modify the program as needed. Such procedures included the preparation and administration of surveys and other methods to measure perceptions of the company's employee relations environment.

All the foregoing elements of a human resources strategy will be helpful. My experience has taught me that it is critical for supervisors to know what their employees are like and whom to hire. It is equally critical that the employees identify with the company and become part of its culture.

One well-known company successfully integrated its employees into its operations and culture. When management told the employees that it wanted to maintain a democratic organization and to hear from the employees, it meant exactly that. In order to encourage the employees to participate in both their own and the company's future, it circulated several memoranda establishing various ways in which management and the employees could communicate with each other. Here are samples of their memoranda:

Speak Up System — The company is committed to communicating with each individual on a one-to-one basis. This communication system will enable you to feel comfortable expressing your feelings to other company team members. This system exists because we believe that you have valuable things to say and we want to hear them. Our committment to listening to you is shared throughout our organization.

Your Supervisor — Your supervisors are a main source of information and instruction. They are responsible for keeping you informed about everything that can affect your job and your performance at the company. You are encouraged to speak with your supervisor about any problem or concern you have which is affecting your job. Your supervisor will do whatever is possible to correct those problems or concerns. Our work philosophy encourages you and your supervisor to work closely together and to communicate openly and honestly with each other.

Employee Assistance Representative — The major responsibility of the Employee Assistance Representative (EAR) is to help resolve any conflicts or complaints that may arise. You should feel free to discuss anything with the EAR if, after speaking with your immediate supervisor, you feel that further conversations with a company team member would be helpful. The EAR is an advisor who is available to assist you in any way he or she can. It is still our intent that you discuss any problems you may have with your immediate supervisor. If for some reason this is not possible, the problem or concern can be discussed confidentially with the EAR.

No-Door — Every level of plant management in the company is eager to help resolve any problem or concern you may have. If, after speaking with your supervisor or the EAR, you still have a question or concern, please speak with the plant manager.

If, after speaking with one or more of these individuals, you still feel that your problem or concern has not been adequately resolved, you should contact the human resources manager. He or she will respond to you directly.

We are sincerely interested in finding out what your views and feelings are and there will never be any reprisals for voicing your concerns.

Again, we encourage each of you to first utilize your supervisor in discussing any concern or problem. However, if for some reason this is not possible, please contact any of the individuals noted above.

Speak Up Meetings — Periodically, members of management will meet with you and other company employees in small groups to discuss various topics. These meetings will give you an opportunity to discuss any concerns or suggestions you may have, as well as keep you informed of important events.

Your supervisor will regularly hold a departmental meeting and you should freely discuss any concerns or suggestions you may have during these meetings.

In addition, quarterly meetings with company management representatives will be held and you are encouraged to discuss any problems, suggestions, ideas, etc. you may have with senior management.

If you should ever feel that a meeting of the employees in your department or section would be helpful, you should contact the human resources manager, the EAR, or the plant manager.

We Can Work It Out — We hope that you will be able to resolve any questions or problems you may have through the informal communications channels described heretofore. However, if you should ever feel that your question or problem needs to be addressed more formally, "We Can Work It Out" is another method to communicate your

problems or concerns. "We Can Work It Out" is the
company's formal problem-resolution process. This
procedure gives you the right to discuss your concerns with
several levels of management.

In the normal operation of any facility, problems or
questions may arise. In addition, rumors often circulate that
may cause a misunderstanding. In most instances, your
supervisor will be able to give you a prompt answer to your
questions and will assist you in solving your problems.
However, your supervisor can only help if you make your
problem known. Should you feel you are being treated
unfairly or that a problem is not being handled properly or
that you need a question answered, you are encouraged to
use the following policy:

First, should a problem arise, we urge you to have a frank
discussion with your supervisor before it affects your work or
perhaps upsets others. Your supervisor has a responsibility to
both you and the facility to solve problems as they arise;
however, without your help your supervisor many not even
be aware that a problem exists.

Second, if the problem remains unresolved, request a meeting with your department or operations manager, who will
investigate the matter and respond to you within one week.

Third, if the problem remains unsolved, request a meeting
with the human resources manager, who will investigate the
matter and respond to you within one week.

Fourth, if you have utilized the first three steps to resolve
your problem and still feel it is unresolved, you may obtain a
complete review of the matter by a committee of three per-
sons not involved in your department or the dispute. You
may select members of this committee from a panel of supervisors and management whose names can be obtained from
the human resources office.

The human resources office will also provide you with a
formal request-for-review form, which must be completed
and returned to the human resources office within twenty-
one days of the date of the incident.

Bulletin Boards — Communication is very important to the success of the company. In addition to the communication channels discussed previously, there are other avenues of communication of which you should be aware. In particular, bulletin boards are placed in various locations throughout the plant. They will carry both routine messages as well as important announcements about holidays, paycheck distribution, training programs, employee meetings, and special employee activities. "Hot News" items will also be posted on colored paper. Please check the bulletin boards located near the pay phones and in the hallway to the main sales office.

Your Ideas — The company wants your ideas and suggestions. Suggestions are welcomed on any subject, especially quality, safety, and methods to save labor, money, energy, time, and materials.

What should you do if you have an idea or suggestions? First and perhaps the most direct approach, would be to discuss your suggestions with your supervisor. Your supervisor may be able to implement your suggestion directly, or you and your supervisor may work to refine your idea so that it may be presented to upper management for implementation. If you prefer, you may present your idea directly to upper management.

Finally, you can always drop your suggestion in one of the suggestion boxes located throughout the plant. Although it is not necessary for you to sign your suggestion, we will not be able to respond to you personally if it is not signed. Responses to all suggestions will, however, be posted on colored paper on the bulletin boards.

Surveys — Periodically, you will be asked to participate in an employee survey which will be conducted on a plant-wide basis by outside consultants. These surveys will be anonymous and voluntary. They provide an opportunity to give management feedback concerning your wants, needs, and desires, and it is hoped that you will view them as a serious opportunity to frankly evaluate the company's work environment.

With your help, we believe these surveys will be a valuable source of information in our constant efforts to improve the quality of work life at the company.

Employee Performance Review — The company's supervisors have heavy responsibilities, especially for quality of products, productivity, and cost containment. No supervisor can do the job alone, and each supervisor needs the help of well-trained, highly efficient, highly qualified, and highly motivated team members.

One of your supervisor's most important responsibilities is your growth and development. Newly hired and newly promoted employees will receive a performance review within the first ninety days of their employment. Thereafter, at least once every ninety days, your supervisor is required to make a written review of your performance on such items as attendance, job skills, productivity, initiative, safety consciousness, and growth potential. During these reviews you and your supervisor will discuss your job performance and plan for your continued development.

It is the company's policy to reward dedicated, qualified employees with pay increases based on performance reviews. At the time of each performance review you will be eligible for additional merit increases. Generally, pay increases will be increments of $.25 per hour, until you reach the maximum wage rate of your job classification. However, performance review time frames may be accelerated and dollar amounts may be increased to recognize and reward superior performance.

Once you reach the current maximum wage rate of your job classification, your performance will be evaluated every six months. If changes in the rate range are indicated, as a result of our periodic industry surveys, appropriate adjustments may be made to the rate ranges and individual rates.

If it is determined that an increase is not merited at the time of the performance review, your supervisor will work closely with you for up to an additional thirty days to help you merit an increase. If after thirty days no improvement is shown, your employment status will be reevaluated. You will be given the support and guidance necessary to help you merit a pay increase.

Even though performance reviews will be completed within the first ninety days of hire and/or promotion and each ninety days thereafter, your supervisor may conduct frequent informal reviews to provide you with any necessary guidance. Whenever you have a question about how you are doing on the job, ask your supervisor. Your performance will be discussed with you at any time and it is not necessary to wait until the formal evaluation process. We all have a need to know "how we are doing."

To assist your supervisor in reviewing your performance, an employee performance review format has been developed. You have an essential role in your performance review which is intended to be an effective two-way communication process. Prior to meeting with your supervisor, your supervisor will request that you complete a performance review form.

Your supervisor will also complete a performance review form. At the time of the performance review, you and your supervisor will discuss your performance, based upon the evaluations both you and your supervisor have prepared. Together, you and your supervisor will plan for your continued growth and development.

* * *

Why all these memoranda? Are all of them necessary to maintain a healthy employee relations climate? Yes, they certainly are.

In most cases, an attempt to organize a particular company starts not from the union but from within the plant. The most common reason a union will try to organize a plant is that the employees have asked for the union's aid to correct what they feel are unfair or inequitable employer policies or practices. That's why intensive efforts to establish good human resources practices are the best way of keeping a union out.

Policy changes or incidents which management views as solid business practices — such as a temporary layoff for a portion of the work force, refusal to give raises or extra benefits, discharging some employees — may well cause certain employees to seek union help if these changes aren't explained or are misunderstood. Quite often inadequate communications between management and workers is the cause of unpleasant incidents which prompt employees to seek help from unions. Sometimes the precipitating incident may be nothing more than a single employee's conviction that he has been treated unfairly. In most instances, however, a general feeling of dissatisfaction, rather than one particular incident, will push employees to seek outside aid.

If management becomes aware of employee unrest over a particular incident or senses a growing feeling of dissatisfaction by a number of employees, it is preferable to spend the time and money to correct the situation promptly rather than risk the cost of a potential organization drive.

Once the union is contacted by the unhappy employee or employees, it will make an informal investigation to determine whether an organizational drive makes sense. If the union organizer finds a receptive atmosphere in which a few workers are willing to help the union in the campaign, it will launch the drive. Even if the union organizer doesn't find many willing employees to help him, he may attempt to create a receptive atmosphere for the campaign by convincing a small group of workers to help on behalf of the union. The organizer may tempt those employees with money or promises of jobs as union stewards and of guaranteed seniority. The union will tell those employees that as stewards with guaranteed seniority they will never be fired after the union wins. If the employees agree to help, the campaign is touched off.

To repeat, it's crucial for the employer to realize that a good employer-employee relationship and sound working conditions are the surest ways to prevent the unionization of his plant or company. The employer who is best able to resist unionization is the one who makes certain that fair personnel policies are an important part of his management.

That aside, there are other matters to be considered by companies eager to remain nonunion.

How to Keep the Union at Bay

Employer Credibility — Union organizers focus on employee discontent with wages, benefits, and job security. They also focus on a perceived need of the workers for protection from the caprice of management and for a voice which can effectively advocate the employees' viewpoint. An employer who has established and maintains credibility with his employees won't have any union problems. To accomplish this, he must first have a disciplinary system which is carried out in a fair and uniform manner. Work rules should be easily understood and should either be posted in a place where employees often congregate or be disseminated in some other way so that all know what the rules are. Disciplinary action should be corrective rather than punitive. When a rule is reasonably and fairly imposed the employee who has knowingly violated the rule is less likely to protest or feel resentful.

All levels of management should avoid appearing to favor some workers over others. Once employees feel that management doesn't treat everyone the same, the quality of work the non-favorites deliver can drop precipitously. They soon feel that unionization is the only way they can eliminate favoritism.

An adequate wage and benefit package is another important way to establish credibility. Employers should take pains to become aware of area standards, wages and benefits offered at comparable area plants, and then should compare theirs with those. If the employer lags much behind, there's a good chance for labor unhappiness.

The best means of quelling wage and benefits dissension is to inform employees of the company's true financial state. In one case, a union organizer deliberately misrepresented a company's financial situation. He said that it earned 13 percent on sales, with net profits in the millions. The actual figure was only about 3 percent and the profit was only about $250,000. The employees voted to organize. Management had not kept the employees informed, and by the time of the election it was too late to correct the misrepresentation made by the union. A consistent policy of communication between management and labor will usually quiet rumors and build trust among all workers.

Employee Selection — If an employer wants to have a content, efficient work force, he should select employees well suited in training, skill, and temperament. Obviously, an employee performing duties which satisfy his needs and desires is likely to be pro-company. Employers should seek employees who demonstrate loyalty and motivation.

Since the best way of evaluating employees is by observing them on the job, this can be accomplished by substituting one employee for another in different positions when this is feasible and when part-time, student, or summer employees are hired. But if on-the-job observation isn't workable, other methods are available. These include performance tests, in which the ability to perform specific job requirements is tested and scored; biographical information; testing specialized knowledge of skills, such as accounting, engineering, marketing; interviews and references.

Interviews are strategic. They are opportune for providing the applicant with a realistic appraisal of his future job. And they also offer an opportunity to question the applicant about any discrepancies among his statements and application and the background check conducted by the employer. It's especially important that the interviewer learn as much as possible about the applicant. Many unions send their own people as job applicants to a plant that they want to organize. It's very worthwhile that the screening process include questions about the applicant's previous employment and why he or she left. A warning signal that an applicant may be a professional union organizer might be the applicant's willingness to accept a significant cut in pay from his previous job since it is possible that his income is being supplemented by the union. But, under no circumstances, may an employer lawfully ask about a prospective employee's union sentiments or affiliation. This would violate the provisions of the Labor Management Relations Act which does not permit an employer "to interfere with, restrain or coerce employees in the exercise of the rights guaranteed in Section 7."

After the employee is hired, the employee selection process doesn't end. A sixty- to ninety-day trial period is recommended. As this period comes to an end, the supervisor should review the employee's performance and recommend retention, transfer, or dismissal.

Reception and orientation are vital for integrating new employees into the company. Employees are most impressionable on their first workday. So to ensure that a new employee is promptly acclimated to the new job and surroundings, the employee should be involved in some sort of welcoming activity. A co-worker might be appointed to show him around the plant and introduce him to fellow employees. A training program should be maintained to ensure that new employees learn how to perform adequately. In such a program, work rules should be clearly set forth so that new employees know exactly what is expected.

If the new employee is left completely to his own resources, he will inevitably make mistakes and suffer from them. He will probably blame the company for its failure to train him properly.

Well-conceived reception and training programs, therefore, are extremely important for any company that wants to chart its own course, free of unions. An employee who identifies closely with the company will be less receptive to outside appeals than one who feels isolated from his co-workers and management. Reception and training programs should, therefore, be used to make the new employee feel he is part of the company as soon as he arrives.

Another key to the worker's continued happiness is placement in a job which satisfies him. The employer should use a "skills file" to help place already hired personnel in the most suitable jobs. This file ought to include the experience and skills of all employees. As vacancies occur, the company can refer to the skills file to seek out qualified personnel among its existing staff, thus saving the expense of recruitment.

Supervisor Training — Supervisors most vividly symbolize a company in the eyes of employees. Since the supervisor holds immediate power over almost every phase of an employee's job, he is the one person who can most help or hurt a company's image.

Supervisors should be adequately trained to prepare them for such a crucial role. However, employers frequently make the mistake of limiting supervisory training to the day-to-day operations that the supervisors oversee. A supervisor's training should also include instruction in the psychology of dealing with employees. The supervisor's inability to treat employees in a sensitive, responsive manner will contribute significantly to employee unrest and therefore will increase the likelihood of a union organizing drive.

Employers should delegate as much responsibility to supervisors as is practical and also should make certain that the supervisors fully understand the exact scope of their authority and how it should be applied. This raises the matter of how far the boss should back up his supervisors. He should support their decisions so as to create respect for those decisions among employees. He should also not hesitate to correct a supervisor's action if it appears to be wrong, unwise, or hasty.

It is extremely important that the employees do not feel intimidated by supervisors. Each employee must feel that he can approach his supervisor freely with any problems. Employees will feel at ease in approaching their superiors if a percentage of supervisors has been promoted from the ranks. Needless to say, this should be done on an impartial basis of merit and seniority. The concept of upward mobility is a good way of maintaining employee morale.

Good Working Conditions — Management too often ignores working conditions, yet they immediately and constantly affect employee morale. Dissatisfaction with physical conditions and the nature of daily assignments can stir union sympathy as much as any other factor. As a result, employers should take pains to establish and maintain a proper working environment.

Job satisfaction is a core factor in achieving satisfactory working conditions. Ideally, every employee should feel that his job is vital to the facility's overall operation. Employers, therefore, should do their best to instill this feeling of functional importance in every employee and to create within him a sense of pride in his work. It is certainly a unique employee who takes pride in his work without management reinforcement.

Encouraging high performance standards and maintaining performance records instills pride. When an employee has undertaken new responsibilities or has performed assignments in an above-average fashion, he should be rewarded accordingly. Merit raises are part of that process, while periodic reviews of job performance can also help to sustain employee pride.

Certain jobs exist in companies in which it will be difficult, if not impossible, to instill pride. Labor specialists call them "soft spots." Due to their excessively onerous or repetitive nature, special attention should be directed toward making these positions as palatable as possible. People employed for these jobs should be given ample break periods and, wherever possible, the positions should be rotated to break their monotony.

All work areas, of course, should be kept clean and free of hazards, according to the standards of the Occupational Safety and

Health Act. When workers believe that they are risking their physical well-being at work, they are almost certain to be dissatisfied and restive. Conversely, scrupulously clean and safe conditions have proven to be a genuine source of satisfaction among employees.

The employees' general comfort should certainly not be overlooked. Work areas should be well-lit and well-ventilated. Toilet facilities should be accessible and clean. Many employers have been experimenting with recreational centers on company premises, including such amenities as pools, game rooms, and lounges, for after-hours enjoyment. Hallmark Cards, for example, maintains a large recreational facility for employees. The annual fee is very nominal and executives have no more right to the facility than employees. Where such resources are available, employees seem to appreciate them greatly.

Grievance Procedure — Employees should have a formalized procedure for filing grievances in addition to periodic group meetings and the suggestion box. In a procedure based on the chain of command, the employee with a grievance goes first to his immediate supervisor. If the employee isn't satisfied with the supervisor's handling of the problem, he should be able to state his objection to someone at a higher managerial level. This step should lead to others, ultimately even to the highest level of management.

It's recommended that every person who reviews the employee's grievance provide a written statement specifying reasons for his decision. If the employee understands the company's rules and how they apply to his case, he is less likely to protest management's ultimate decision.

Competitive Wage-Benefit Package — The employer shouldn't allow his wage-benefit package to fall behind industry or regional norms. He should endeavor to keep his entire package comparable to the area standards, not only within his particular industry but within similar industries. Yet an employer may be forced to offer a package which is below par in some aspects. If that's the case, candor is the best policy. If it's a question of too much expense, the employer must explain to his employees why he can't afford to give them greater benefits at that time. He should be certain to tell them that their package will increase as the company's economic status improves.

Should seniority or merit determine wage scales and classification? Every employer has a goal of optimum productivity. By rewarding good performance with a salary increase or bonus, he provides incentives to his employees to work and perform better. If the employee who conscientiously strives to excel finds, instead of rewards, a salary no better than that given to his most mediocre colleague, he can easily become frustrated and lose interest. Thus, merit should play some part in determining the pay of employees.

At the same time, the appeal of seniority attracts many workers to the union fold. Afraid that years of work and dedication will go unnoticed, they seek the lure of security and forego the opportunity for merit raises in favor of uniform wage scales based on seniority. It's questionable that security really works in favor of most employees. But its widespread appeal as a demand by unions makes it much too important to ignore.

Management should note that where jobs are routine and the employees who perform them can be easily replaced, individual merit has little meaning. Where such a situation exists, a company may well be able to achieve maximum productivity by using some form of seniority.

In general, the best wage scale policy is one which attempts to balance the goal of maximum productivity with the claims of seniority. In jobs where employee skill or performance are measurable and will contribute to increased efficiency and productivity if rewarded, wage scales should reflect both seniority and merit. Where jobs are routine and individual merit has little meaning, length of service may be the best method of determining wage scales.

* * *

What, then, is the crux of maintaining loyal, pro-company employees? Sound management techniques. Common sense. Consideration for other people. These three principles are a powerful combination. Anything less just won't work.

CHAPTER XIV

COLLECTIVE LEADERSHIP VS. COLLECTIVE BARGAINING

"The by-products of employee involvement were improved productivity, better quality products, and a more wholesome quality of life in the workplace."

The Scenario Revisited

The President awoke at 2:47 A.M. Lying there, his lean, spare form as relaxed as he could keep it, he wondered what had awakened him. He felt secure on the foreign affairs level. But the domestic situation, especially after what he had learned that night . . .

Sighing inwardly, he lit a cigarette, surprised by the shaky feeling in the pit of his stomach. He hated to do it, but he picked up the telephone and woke both the White House chief of staff and the press secretary. During the conference call he asked them to meet him for breakfast at 6:45 and to be prepared for a tough day.

At breakfast the President, who liked to pride himself on some accurate instincts about people, was certain that his two assistants hadn't compared notes. They ate silently and finished a little after seven. The President leaned back and said, "Gentlemen, some of the most depressing news on the home front we have had in years is due out today. Do you know what it is?"

The chief of staff, a former infantry general, didn't hesitate. "The trade balance for the latest quarter will show the biggest gap in recent history, Mr. President," he said.

"The latest reading on industrial productivity," said the press secretary, "indicates a considerable slip."

The President nodded dourly. "I see that you two men have been keeping in touch — as you should. But is there anything else?"

Both shrugged.

"I wish that were all the bad news we will hear today. But unfortunately, gentlemen, it isn't. Last night, before I retired," he resumed, "I called the chairman of the Fed. He confidentially informed me that all the indications this afternoon are that the dollar will begin to increase against most of the major money markets which will probably culminate in a few weeks in a 25 percent rise against foreign currencies. Do you gentlemen know what that means? It means that imports will jump suddenly to an all-time high," he told them. "The trade balance will get worse. Industrial output will go even lower. And all that will lead to the highest unemployment we have had in at least five years."

They were all silent, letting the facts and the projections sink in. Finally, the President said harshly, "We must do something to head off the unfortunate reaction of all this bad news. There will be a political storm whether we don't or we do. But regardless, we've got to act. And fast."

"What are your instructions, Mr. President" the chief of staff asked.

"Here is what we must do," the President said. "And damn quietly too. We won't tell the media anything until it's all over and we have the advantage of a *fait accompli*, a surprise sealed in action. Now, listen to me. . . ."

Later that morning tight-lipped messengers personally handed a Presidential summons to twelve men in high places in the private sector. Six were the nation's corporate leaders, including the chairmen of the boards of General Motors, American Telephone &

Telegraph, and Exxon Corporation. The others were the leaders of the union movement, including the presidents of the AFL-CIO, the International Brotherhood of Teamsters, and the Communications Workers of America. At six that evening, the twelve sat with hardly concealed concern in a rarely used room of the White House, cleared and sealed off for security, with the President, the chief of staff, and the press secretary. Grimly the President studied each man, wondering if they were capable of meeting the demands he would soon put on them.

"Gentlemen, out in my neck of the Nevada plains there's an ol' sayin' that when a rattlesnake comes at you," he began, "you don't stand there considerin' the situation. You cut off its damn head fast as you can." Quickly he explained the situation as he had described it at breakfast. General Motors' chairman listened carefully, his heart pounding as he sensed what was coming. He threw a glance at the grizzled AFL-CIO chief, who had fought him at every turn. The union leader held his gaze with a hard one of his own. The strange thing, he realized, is that the two of them came from the same sort of industrial town, the offspring of poor working families. Of any two men on both sides of the bargaining table, they should have gotten along. But now the President, after a lapse in which he had stared angrily at the floor, spoke again.

"The question, my friends, is how we are goin' to cut off the head of this rattlesnake." He paused again. Funny how both sides had lined up in kind, the labor men on one side of the table, management on the other. Would they, could they, get together, he wondered. The President, inured to so many confrontations in his battle-scarred political career, swallowed audibly. "There's only one way left to us, friends," he said. "We need a positive act for public relations purposes when the American public sees the dollar skyrocket into outer space. But, more important, my fellow Americans, we need an irrefutable, irrevocable national program. We need some strong assurance that you in management and you in labor will pull together from now on for the good of the U.S. of A. In short, gentlemen, I want a national program in which all of you will commit yourselves to any and all actions necessary to improve our national productivity, our international trade balance, the stability of the dollar, our national competitive ability, and our employment rate. Gentlemen, let me put it to you this way. I want you to wrap yourselves in the American flag!"

He leaned back, opening the bottom drawer of the desk slightly in the process, and watched their reaction. They were all staring at one another in dismay, evidently having heard much more of a sweeping declaration than they had anticipated. No one spoke immediately.

Finally, the GM executive cleared his throat. "Sir, I am not at all sure that you will be able to obtain unity in our industry," he said, "particularly with the intense competition already facing us from Japan. As to our attitude toward organized labor, sir, that could be even more sticky."

The AFL-CIO chief would not be jockeyed out of position. "Mr. President," he said, "without knowing exactly what we will be called upon to commit ourselves to in this national program, I cannot help wondering if you will not be asking the labor movement to cooperate by cutting off its fingers and its toes."

Suddenly they were all talking. Glancing at his watch and opening the desk drawer a little further, the President couldn't help noting that they were pulling out all stops, engaging in every conceivable polemic against the other side. If they could only apply that energy to working together in the national interest. After ten minutes he held up his hand. "I am asking you to volunteer for a movement to help this country get out of an economic dungpit. I myself could take action that you would surely despise. I could ask the Congress to enact wage and price controls. They have never really worked, have they? But I would take that step to penalize all of you. I could instruct my investigative agencies, the SEC, Justice, the FTC, and most of the other regulatory agencies, to pursue a tough new policy toward business and make all your lives miserable. I could make the Labor Department and the NLRB adopt much more rigid policies and put the unions through the wringer. But I do not intend to. I do intend to urge you most forcefully to do what's right for this country while we still have time, before we become not a second-rate power but a third or fourth."

In the long silence which followed, the breathing in the room was palpable. But doubt lingered on most faces. What the hell did this ex-cowboy really want? Finally, the GM chairman, normally a suave, diplomatic executive with a core of steel, asked in a quavering voice, "Mr. President, in practical terms, what do you want us to do?"

The chief executive nodded, glad it had come down to that.

"What I want from all of you patriotic Americans are your signatures on a new management-labor manifesto that will pledge your cooperation and that of your organizations to obtain those goals I mentioned earlier. It will include your commitment to a number of steps which will avoid all the hurdles which have created a terrible rift between business and labor all these past years. They will be a bitter pill for both sides to swallow. I will create a new cabinet rank, say, a Secretary of Management-Labor Relations, who will be the final arbiter—next to me, of course—to summarily settle any disputes as they arise. And every decision will be binding on all of you so that we can get ahead with the business of this country once more."

Many questions were thrown at him, one after another, without allowing him the chance to reply. Again he held up his hand. "Gentlemen, I will not give any specifics at this time. I will tell you that everything you fear will probably be listed in the manifesto. But each side will be called upon to sacrifice equally."

Silence again. Glancing at his watch, the President took a deep breath and said, "Gentlemen, as you know, one of the most potentially violent confrontations was due to happen a few minutes ago in South Carolina. The Rubber and Tire Workers Union had threatened to mass picket a nonunion plant in a little town down there after months of organizing. The town authorities, the National Guard, the local police, have all pledged to stop any confrontation resulting from the picketing which, in fact, violates local statutes. Last night I dispatched the Secretary of Labor to fly down and give us a personal report because I had a feeling that this situation would tell us more than I could possibly tell you. He is standing by down there and I will put him on the speakerphone."

In moments the Labor Secretary's voice filled the room with an emotion-racked recitation. "Mr. President, this is one of the worst scenes I can remember in all my years! A blood-bath! Four people are dead, three union men and the assistant plant manager! The pickets tried to break down the iron fence and the plant security people fired from inside, the National Guard from outside. I estimate more than twenty wounded, maybe twice that many when the smoke clears!"

The President cut him off and stared with sad eyes at the

twelve men in the room. But suddenly there was pandemonium. The union contingent rose in its seats, shouting and cursing at the management representatives. The latter got up too, yelling and accusing in kind. The President leaned back, sighing again. He had miscalculated. He had planned the Labor Secretary's expected report from the scene as a demonstration of how explosive the current situation could be, hoping that it would show them that there could be only one way. But instead it had ignited the same old angers and charges.

Something clicked deeply within the President. He pulled the desk drawer wide open, reached in, and pulled out an old but working Colt .45. Rising, he carefully aimed the barrel at a corner of the ceiling and pulled the trigger. The thunder of the gunshot and the accompanying clatter of falling plaster threw a shock wave through the room. Utter silence followed. The President sat down and replaced the revolver in the drawer. The White House security wouldn't come storming in. He had alerted the security chief early that morning of the eventuality. But he knew that he would be facing some stormy music for a while, accused of theatrics and melodrama. But the ploy had been effective before. Some said that he had won his first nomination to the Presidency when he had fired the Colt from the rostrum of the national convention. He had, then, brought down a huge floating balloon in order to symbolize his determination to lead the country with action, not words.

He sat for another moment or two, a tiny smile laying on his lips and gazed at everyone. "Well, gentlemen," he said, "are we ready to conclude this little roundup? I'm asking you for once to do something for *all of us*, not just for yourselves and your own constituents." He leaned across the desk. "Who, my fellow Americans, will make the first gesture?"

He was asking for a lot, he knew, when he asked these men to suddenly cast off the habits and prejudices of a lifetime. Several hundred thunderous heartbeats later there was a stirring, a breaking up of the pantomime of shock. Almost unconsciously, as they still faced each other, the GM chairman and the AFL-CIO chief were softly punching each other's shoulder and grinning.

"You old company buster," said the GM chief.

"You old union buster," said the union president.

"What do you say?"

"What do *you* say?"

Just as suddenly both men were clasping each other and pounding each other's back. Within moments everyone else was doing the same. Long decades of management-labor strife and rancor were melting away and personal animosities and long-harbored antagonisms didn't seem to mean anything. Soon there wasn't a dry eye left in the room, including those of the President who suspected that his happy tears could have been the biggest of all.

Fantasy, you say? Melodramatic? Apocryphal? Perhaps. But I can't help wondering how far this scenario is from reality. A blink of the eye? A twist of fate? Who can say?

The Issues, as Before

After two years of working on this book, after some twenty years of experience, and after so much exposure to the trauma and drama of the management-labor field, I can only conclude that correction must come from within. Government of course can attempt to pressure both management and labor to modify their behavior. But it simply won't work unless fundamental attitudes and beliefs change as well. It's like the mortally ill patient who is saved for the time being by the fantastic medication but really doesn't want to stay well. Life-prolonging devices can only carry him semi-lifelessly and unwillingly along until the inevitable happens.

That, in essence, is my conviction about the ability of management and labor to get together, drop their shibboleths and prejudices of the past, and unite to achieve a common goal. My purpose in writing this book has been only to bring all the facts together and to combine those facts with the observations of my life in the negotiating field. To me, there seems to be no other option, no other alternative. But it is up to those many enlightened people in each field to rouse themselves and to finally take the initiative to meet the adversary at least halfway. No one — absolutely no one else — can do it for them.

What are the basic urgencies which so desperately cry out for it?

If the nation's industrial machine is to be renewed, if the economy is to be set on a constructive course beyond a favorable blip here or there, the joining of minds and purposes for a common strategy is essential. The reverse is untenable because it will lead inevitably to economic and political stagnation.

A top priority must be to develop a strategy for economic growth which will allow the United States to compete in the emerging sectors of the economy, such as biotechnology, telecommunications, robotics, and computerization.

Better labor relations will facilitate the adoption of new technologies by mature industries and foster discovery, production, and growth by small companies.

Japan and West Germany have both successfully undergone a renewed national commitment. So the U.S., as a constitutional democracy, should be able to undertake such a task through either individual acts, the legislative process, or both.

Is our nation so locked into its hidebound ways, its protective traits for its pluralistic segments, that a call for common purpose is just a wasted effort? That doesn't seem to be the case, judging by the homogeneity and unity of efforts during World Wars I and II, the gasoline crunch of the mid-1970s, and other difficult times. When the issues are bared, we have all been gratified to find that we live in a self-correcting society.

Can it happen again? Is there, perhaps, already a sense of economic renewal, of the awareness of a common confrontation of issues, stirring in the land? Are management and labor, here and there, looking at one another and sensing that it is time to change and move together on common problems?

Perhaps, because a vacuum exists and vacuums, we are told, are always filled.

But that can only happen when management, labor, and the government take off their blinders to focus on what is more important than politics, to focus on mutual rather than separate benefit, and especially to focus on the future instead of the past.

Already, there are some promising signs in 1985 that we are becoming more attuned to reality than fantasy.

More companies and unions were involved in participation programs than ever before. Some 2,000 corporations involved their employees in a spectrum of management activities. The by-products of employee involvement were improved productivity, better quality of product, and a more wholesome quality of life in the workplace. Companies which have involved employees in management activities include Hughes Aircraft, General Motors, Lockheed, Ford, Martin Marietta, and Honeywell.

The General Motors Saturn project is a dramatic example of how management and labor can work together. For ninety days a joint management-labor team of 99 people huddled in a concentrated effort to mould a decision to construct a small, fuel-saving, moderately-priced car that could compete on a worldwide basis. In effect, the team was responsible for a $5 billion G.M. investment, one which could have major ramifications for both management and labor.

This new concept of joint management-labor ventures had been worked out by both G.M. and Ford Motor Company and the unions and was included in the 1984 collective bargaining agreements. Both companies had agreed to earmark millions of dollars to develop new business ventures conceived by joint management labor committees.

One could hope, perhaps, after all.

Some Final Words on a Personal Note

This book has taken me a long way. And yet as I complete it, I have the strange feeling of *deja vu*, as though I were still only seventeen and it is only yesterday, a long yesterday ago. It's a warm, satisfying feeling, in a sense, because it means I am not yet jaded, even though I am well past those teen years. Perhaps I feel that way because I don't want ever to lose that dimension of freedom or the youthful hope that things will be better than they are now.

In any professional field, the practitioner can easily become cynical, emotionally or mentally fatigued, or, worse, beaten down by the harsh weight of realities. I trust that will never happen to me because I would then never be able to function in the manner I would like. But, of course, one must always guard against the kind of fatigue that lies in wait for anyone fighting in any arena of any kind anywhere.

I had that sort of challenge recently. I was called in to help a manufacturing company with plants in the U.S. and Canada. It was involved in a difficult economic situation and was having trouble working out a corrective program with the various unions representing its employees. The company had tried to get advice from other lawyers, but all had suggested a nonaggressive policy. Yet the company was in dire straits. What it vitally needed was an action program that would relieve the pressure. It reminded me of my father's situation so many years ago when he had been unable to get the courageous advice he needed to stay alive as a businessman.

When I came into the situation, I thought about it long and hard and decided that there was only one route to take. Calling everyone together, I told them that if they couldn't act as a team, the company had authorized me to say that it would have to close down. Everyone listened because they realized the gravity of the situation. As a result, we drew up a plan in which some of the employees would be laid off and pay scales would be reduced for all the workers. But, once we had the unions' cooperation, we were able to come up with a timetable to return most of the laid-off employees to work. Both sides were clearly asked in urgent terms to cease their external and internal fighting in order to help the company regain its competitive position. The timetable called for a return of many workers within fifteen months and the reinstatement of the former level of wages within thirty-six months.

The union officials at first refused to go along because they said it would embarrass them to agree to concessions for promises that they weren't sure would be followed up with action. But we made certain that management remained totally up-front, candid, and cooperative in its disclosures to the union. So the compact was reached and the deal was made.

The risk remained for the union, of course. But management was sincere and the prognosis was bright.

I walked away from all that with a very positive feeling. Twenty years ago it probably wouldn't have been possible. At least I hadn't seen many situations like this before and not too many times since. But I am witnessing it now and then — the mutual faith to carry out a mutual goal — and I must admit it's almost like seeing a pleasant dream become a reality. Is it possible, as I mentioned earlier, that there's a sense of management-labor cooperation stirring in the land? One can only seek it, urge it — and pray.

In taking the position of asking both employers and unions to cooperate for a joint objective, I know that there are those who will scoff at the sincerity of a management attorney asking labor to bend, to give up its traditionally unreasonable demands, to bite the bullet if it has to in order to keep a company alive and jobs secure. But I am also asking management to bend, to give up its unreasonable demands, and to bite the bullet if necessary to stay alive and keep jobs secure. It's a prescription for courage in a time when only courage will do.

In that sense, I have dedicated my professional life to clearing the air between the protagonists in the management-labor field, not taking the easy, complacent, unproductive stances that others may have seen fit to take. And I would like to carry on the challenge, not just in this country but abroad, too. The challenge, it's obvious to me, has only just begun and it's far too early for anyone to be complacent.

There's just too much at stake. And too little time left to achieve it.

INDEX

A & P, 19, 106, 139
Airline Pilots Association, 36, 144
Albus, James, 168
American Federation of Labor
  and Congress of Industrial
  Organizations (AFL-CIO), 8-9,
  14, 22, 38, 52, 68, 70, 71, 97,
  110, 118, 125, 144, 148-149,
  156, 203-04; Union of Hospital
  and Health Care Employees,
  RWSDU, AFL-CIO, District
  1199C, 27
American Telephone and
  Telegraph Company, 111, 202-
  03
Anderson, Robert, 65
Anderson-Saxon Group, 67
Aron, Paul H., 165-66
Asian countries, wage laws, 56
Australia, wage laws, 56

Bankruptcy Code, 143, 44
Barbero, Frank, 120
Belgium, wage laws, 55
Bennett, Harry, 156
Bieber, Owen, 149
Bildisco Manufacturing Com-
  pany, 145-46
Blacks in work force, 83, 91-95
  99-105, 118, 155, 156
Blandish, Eddie, 110

Blandish, Paul, 110
Borman, Frank, 19
Bureau of National Affiars, 21,
  67; *Employee Relations Weekly*,
  180
Business Council, 63
Business-Higher Education
  Forum, 65
Business Week, 64

Canada, wage laws, 56; govern-
  ment involvement in labor
  relations, 58-59
Carter, President Jimmy, 43
Chamber of Commerce. *See*
  United States Chamber of
  Commerce
Chrysler Corporation, 14, 20,
  149, 165
Communications Workers of
  America, 72, 203, 111
Communist countries, wage laws,
  55
Conference Board, 85, 148
Congress of American Industry.
  See National Association of
  Manufacturers
Continental Airlines, 126, 145

Dainichi Machinery Company,
  166
Daiwa Securities America, Inc.
  165
Denmark, wage laws, 55
Detroit, 56-57

Donahue, Phil, 11; the *Donahue* show, 120-121
Duffy, Henry, 144
Dunlop, John T., 22
Du Pont. *See* E.I. Du Pont de Nemours & Company

E.I. Du Pont de Nemours & Company, 64
Eastern Airlines, 19, 28
Ekonomisuto, 168
Engelberger, Joseph F., 169
England. *See* Great Britain
Equal Employment Opportunity Act, 42
Equal Employment Opportunity Commission, 48
Estreicher, Samuel, 52-53
Evans, James H., 63-64
Exxon Corporation, 203

Face the Nation, 155
Federal Labor Act, 8
Federal Mediation and Concilliation Service, 48, 54, 123
Federal minimum wage, 42, 53-54
Federal Public Contracts Act, 54
Fier, Donald, 36
Ford, Henry, 156
Ford Motor Company, 19-21, 149, 209
France, wage laws, 55; government involvement in labor relations, 58, 60; labor force, 96; management, 144
Franklin, Benjamin, vii
Fraser, Douglas, 38, 154
Freedom of Information Act, 61
Freeman, Aubrey, 148

General Electric Company, 86-87

General Motors Corporation, 19-21, 44, 64, 110, 149, 165, 169, 202-04, 209; dealership in Mt. Holly, NJ, 5
Gold, Laurence, 144-45
Gompers, Samuel, 74, 77
Gotbaum, Victor, 146
government involvement in labor relations in other countries, 56-60
Great Atlantic & Pacific Tea Company. *See* A & P
Great Britain, economy, 38; government involvement in labor relations, 58; management, 114
Green Bay Packers, 31
Greenhouse, Steven, 52
Greyhound, 126, 156

Hallmark Cards, 199
Hewlett-Packard Company, 14
Hiroshima, 56
Hispanics in work force, 83, 91-95, 99-106, 118, 155
Hoffenstein, Samuel, 10
Holusha, John, 56-57
Honeywell, 209
Hotel Association of New York, 18
House Task Force on Inflation, 85-86
Hughes Aircraft, 209

Ikehata, Keiji, 167-68
INC. Magazine, 169
India, wage laws, 56
Industry Week, 111, 165
Information Center on International Competitiveness, 66
International Association of Machinists, 11, 68, 144

International Brotherhood of Teamsters, 3-4, 20-21, 22, 24, 27, 44, 46, 50, 67, 70, 130, 145, 203; strike by Mt. Holly, NJ local, 5; Eastern Conference of Teamsters, 25

International Harvester Company, 113

International Ladies Garment Workers Union, 67-68

Italy, wage laws, 55, 58; government involvement in labor relations, 60, management, 114

Japan, management, 39, 144; auto industry, 47, 119-20; wage laws, 55-56, 208; government involvement in labor relations, 60, 84-85; labor force, 96; employee relations, 138; use of robotics, 165-68; *kangan* inventory method, 173

Jasinowski, Jerry J., 149-50

Jefferson, Edward G., 64

Johnson, President Lyndon, 66

Journal of Labor Research, 184

"Just in Time" inventory method, 173

Kirkland, Lane, 13-14, 38, 52, 71, 97, 144, 151, 154

Kohno, Toshio, 166-67

Labor Anti-Racketeering Act, 61

Labor Management Relations Act. *See* Taft-Hartley Act

Labor Relations Board. *See* National Labor Relations Board (NLRB)

Lamston. *See* M.H. Lamston, Inc.

Latin American countries, wage laws, 56

Lazard Freres and Company, 36

Linden, Fabian, 85-86

Litton Industries, 118

Lockheed, 209

Lombardi, Vince, 31

M.H. Lamston, Inc., 115

MacPhail, Lee, 35-36

Martin, Dr. Edith, 167

Master Chef, 126

Master Freight Agreement. *See* National Master Freight Agreement

Matsushita Electric Industrial Company, 165

Mazda, 56

Megatrends, 155

Metro North line, 30

minimum wage. *See* Federal minimum wage

Naisbitt, John, 155, 158

National Association of Manufacturers, 147, 149-50; Congress of American Industry, 86-87

National Bureau of Standards, 168

National Commission on Industrial Competitiveness, 66

National Industrial Recovery Act (NIRA), 53-54

National Labor Relations Act, 53-54

National Labor Relations Board (NLRB), 5, 7-9, 43, 47, 48-52, 54, 58, 76, 80, 83, 99, 118, 122, 125, 145, 204

National Master Freight Agreement, 20, 22, 24, 25

Neal, Dean Phil C., 66

New York Hotel & Motel Trades Council, 17-18

New York Stock Exchange, 12
New York *Times*. 52, 56, 64,
    67,144,145-46, 150
New York University, 52
Newsday, 166
Nissan, 124
Nixon, President Richard, 66
Norris-LaGuardia Act, 54

Occupational Safety and Health
    Act, 198-99
Ohsone, Tetuo, 56
Organization for Economic
    Cooperation and Develop-
    ment, 96
Orientals in U.S. work force, 93,
    96, 155

Pakistan, wage laws, 56
Pan American World Airlines
    (Pan Am), 36
Parade, 154
Philadelphia Inquirer, 112
Players Association, 36
pollution controls, 7
President's Productivity Commis-
    sion, 66
Pulasky, Sandy, 120

quality circles, 39, 84-85, 172-73

Reagan, President Ronald, 11, 30,
    52, 64, 66, 139, 157
Riesel, Victor, 110
Robena Mine, 110, 118
robotics, 64, 75, 121-22, 161-73
Rockwell International Corpora-
    tion, 65
Rosow, Jerome M., 68

Samuel, Howard, 118
Saxon, David S., 65

Schrank, Robert, 154
SEPTA, 29-30
Serrin, William, 67-68
Service Employees International
    Union, 101
South Africa, wage laws, 56
Soviet Union, labor laws, 60;
    use of robotics, 167
Sri Lanka, wage laws, 56
Stahl, Leslie, 155
Standard Oil of Indiana, 11
Stigler, Professor George J., 66
Swearingen, John, 11

TWA, 12
Taft-Hartley Act, 50, 54, 60, 61,
    196
Teamsters. *See* International
    Brotherhood of Teamsters
teenagers in work force. *See*
    youth in work force
Tekulve, Kent, 111
Terkel, Studs, 155-58
Times. See New York *Times*
Toyo Kogyo Company, 56
Toyota, 165
Transport Workers Union, 36

Unimation, Inc., 169
Union of Hospital and Health
    Care Employees, 12, 27
Union Pacific Corporation, 63
Union of South Africa. *See*
    South Africa
unions, harassment, 4, 13; dissen-
    tion within, 6-7, 118, 139, 152-
    53; strikes, 12-13, 17, 29-30,
    36, 50, 104, 113-114, 123;
    changing image, 45, 110, 120-
    121, 183-84; decline in mem-
    bership, 67-69, 87-88, 143;
    organizing, 72, 79-80, 88, 97-

102, 106, 115-16, 194-95
United Airlines, 12
United Auto Workers Union, 14, 20-21, 38, 57, 64, 110, 113, 149, 154, 156
United Electrical Workers Union, 120
United Food and Commmercial Workers International Union, 28, 72, 139, 149
United Mine Workers of America, 68, 110
United Parcel Service, 22
United Rubber Workers of America, 67
United States Chamber of Commerce, 125
United States Shoe Corporation, 115
United Steel Workers of America, 67, 70, 75-76, 140
University of Chicago, 66, 67
University of California, 65
University of Pennsylvania Law School, 4

Villanova University, 4

wage laws in other countries, 55-57

Wagner Act. *See* National Labor Relations Act
Wall Street Journal, 5
Walsh-Healey Act, 54
Warren, Alfred S., Jr., 64
Watergate Investigating Commission, 61
Welch, John F., Jr., 86-87
West Germany, wage laws, 60; labor force, 96; management, 114; auto industry, 120, 208
Williams, Roy, 26
Wilson Foods, 113, 145
Winpisinger, William W., 11, 144, 154, 156
women in work force, 67-68, 82-83, 91-96, 99-103, 118, 115, 156
Work in America Institute, Inc., 68
Working, 155
Wynn, William, 28, 149

Young, John A., 14
Young, Wendall, 139
youth in work force, 81, 92-96, 102-106, 117-118, 156
Yugoslavia, labor laws, 56

Zalvsky, John, 22